The Salt & Pepper Gang

a memoir

KENNETH ARTHUR

 Suncoast Books

ISBN paperback: 978-0-578-80499-6

Cover design: Peter Selgin

Interior typesetting: Vanessa Mendozzi

This book is dedicated to
Donald Ray Price

Chapter One

It's 1972, and I am eight years old. Through the loud song of the cicadas in the trees, I hear my mother call my name. I get up from the Army men I have positioned around dirt clods in the backyard. She tells me to come inside and take a bath, and I want to know why. It's not even dark. She says we are going somewhere. That's good enough for me, so I march toward the house.

When I pull back the shower curtain and step out of the tub, I notice a brochure on the toilet that shows boys wearing cowboy hats and riding horses. It says "Cal Farley's Boys Ranch, established 1939." Panic and fear make me almost unable to move. I dry off and put the towel around me and go to my room. My mother packs my suitcase. She ignores my crying, my pleading, "No, please no," and tells me to hurry and get dressed. I can't because I'm slumping to the ground, bawling, begging her through tears, my hands together in prayer at her feet. It's for my own good, she tells me. She's getting a divorce and I need to be as far away from my father as I can get, she says. I have ten sets of aunts and uncles and twenty-two cousins. Can't I stay with somebody in the family? Her answer is no. It's already been decided. Boys Ranch will take care of me from now on. She will come see me whenever she can.

She drives me to downtown Longview, Texas, to the Continental Trailways bus station, with my three sisters sitting in the back. They cry like it's the end of the world. She makes them stay in the car when she walks me to the bus. I have forty-three cents in a plastic change pouch and a brown paper sack with a banana and a bologna sandwich. We stand under moths and bugs clattering around a light bulb. She gives me her final words. "Sit behind the bus driver. You'll get to Dallas around midnight and will have to change busses. The driver will help you get on the right bus. When you get to Amarillo tomorrow, a man will meet you and take you to Boys Ranch. Don't lose your tickets. Write me letters, okay?"

I beg her, "No, please, no," and hold onto her, but she separates herself from me and I have to go up the steps of the bus. The driver closes the door. I keep thinking my mother is going to come up and tap on it and get his attention, change her mind, and take me off the bus. I look out the windows thinking she has to stop the bus. She's going to stop the bus. She's going to turn around and come running back. But she's walking away, down the sidewalk, toward the car.

The bus starts going. It pulls out and into the street. The big buildings in downtown Longview go by, and then the city goes by. Onto the interstate I go, feeling cast out of my family. I pray to Jesus to take me back home, to wake me up from this dream because it can't be true, this nightmare I'm in. What did I do wrong?

Dallas bus station. Midnight. Over the speaker comes the announcement, "Now boarding for Henrietta, Wichita Falls, Quanah, Childress, Amarillo, Tucumcari, and Albuquerque. Gate Three." I walk to the bus with my suitcase like I'm headed to the gas chamber. Cowboys and old men with turquoise bolo ties make way for me.

I sit behind the bus driver against the window. None of the people getting on look happy at all, the women with their big Texas hair and downcast faces and the men all frowns. It's late, so maybe they're just sleepy. We get going and soon we're on the big road headed out of downtown Dallas. An old lady on the seat across from me keeps staring. Earlier, she told me in the bus station when she saw my chin quivering that everything was going to be all right. She's got a big mole on her face and a long hair sprouting out from it. How does she know everything is going to be all right? Nothing is going to be all right. My chin's quivering again and I ball up my fists and turn to the window. The lights of the Dallas suburbs fly past, the houses and neighborhoods. Why is this happening to me? I'm not a bad person. Everybody else is at home in their beds with their moms and dads. What did I do? Whatever it was, my sisters are worse. But they're not on a bus being shipped off to nowhere. It's just not fair, old lady with the hairy mole who's still staring at me. Thank God when we pull into Henrietta, Texas, she gets off the bus while I pretend to sleep. She pats my head and I feel sorry for thinking about her hairy mole. She probably hates it, and it's not her fault.

I find myself crying sometimes in the night on the bus. It just happens. Mid-morning the next day, a man wearing a cowboy hat and a suit, Mr. Harriman, meets me at the Amarillo bus station and drives me forty miles out to Boys Ranch. I sleep in the back seat. He wakes me when we're nearly there. It's all dirt and rocks. Cactus. Mesquite bushes. Mesas. Mr. Harriman points out the Boys Ranch water tower in the distance. We cross over the dry Canadian River and head down a lonely road toward the ranch nestled under cottonwood trees a mile away.

Going past Boot Hill cemetery, he tells me that gunslingers were buried there back before Boys Ranch existed, back in the Old West when there was a town here named Tascosa that had saloons and gambling halls and hotels, a tiny town centered around just about the only courthouse in the Texas Panhandle. It died and became a ghost town. In 1939, a guy named Cal Farley took in nine boys roaming the streets of Amarillo and put them in the abandoned courthouse, one of the only buildings left standing. Mr. Harriman says that Cal brought in more and more disadvantaged boys over time. That's how Boys Ranch came to be. MGM made a movie about it in 1946, he says.

We drive through the Boys Ranch gate, past a buffalo in a pen and a Texas Longhorn, past a white wooden chapel and the old Tascosa courthouse that has been turned into a museum. We pull up to the dining hall. Twelve to fifteen dogs loiter around. Thirty bicycles lie about, most of them with banana seats and ape hanger handlebars. There's nobody to be seen.

When we go through the doors into the dining hall, I hear the roar of hundreds of people talking and silverware tinkling on dishes. There are 450 people, mostly boys with buzz cuts, sitting eating lunch at fifty round tables in a big open room. They have pork chops and mashed potatoes. Green beans. Buttered rolls. Peach cobbler.

Everybody looks at me carrying my suitcase as I follow Mr. Harriman. He guides me to a table where a man pushes his chair back and stands up to meet me. Rugged and weathered, the man is the size of a building and has a huge gold-and-silver Texas belt buckle. His wife, in a dazzling white nurse's uniform, stands next to him and smiles down at me. Mr. Harriman tells me they are Mr. and Mrs. Price, my dorm parents. I'll be living with them and thir-ty-something boys in Anderson Dorm. He kneels to see me eye to eye and tells me there are fourteen dorms and over four hundred boys here, and Anderson Dorm is one of the best. He says I'm in good hands.

When lunch is over, Mr. Price drives me to the Boys Ranch County Store, where he outfits me with Levi's and work boots and socks and shirts. He takes me to see Mr. Lamont Waldrip, a big man in charge of all kinds of stuff. Mr. Waldrip sits me down at his desk and gives me a little pamphlet and welcomes me to Boys Ranch. He goes into what being a Boys Rancher is all about. It's important, he says, to be respectful, saying yes sir and no sir and yes ma'am and no ma'am; to follow the rules and work hard; and to make good grades and have a good attitude. From there we go over to a lady behind a window, and they tell me I'm at the Boys Ranch bank. The lady hands me a checkbook and she and Mr. Price explain how I'll be given a job and will get paid every month and can write checks for snacks and ice cream at the concession stand or for clothes or a bicycle or whatever I have enough money to buy. I make my first deposit. Forty-three cents.

As Mr. Price gets his cigarette going, we get in his yellow pickup and head toward Anderson Dorm. Dozens of boys stream in all directions, on bicycles, popping wheelies, some running, some strolling along in groups. Dogs are everywhere. We get to the dorm, where he introduces me to Mr. Weddell, the alternate dorm parent, who lives with his wife and children in an apartment built into one side of the dorm. Mr. Price and his family live in the other apartment. Between them is what they call the Big Room, with a fireplace, a pool table, a trophy case, and lots of chairs and couches along the walls. There are six rooms with five or six boys in each, and three bathrooms. They assign me to Room Two and show me my locker and my bunk bed.

I soon find out I'm the youngest and the smallest of the thirty-something boys in the dorm. They initiate me into their ways. One kid asks me, "Have you ever had a wedgie?" I naively say no, and they turn me around, grab the elastic band of my underwear and go to lifting me off the ground with it. Another kid standing there asks, "What about a noogie? Had one of those?" This time I say, "Yes, I have," even though I have no idea what they are talking about. "Good," the kid says. "Here's another one." He gets me in a headlock and now I know what a noogie is, and a Wet Willie. The big boys make me shine their shoes, make their beds, and give them my chocolate milk.

Twice in my first week I get the water torture. I go with other little boys down to the big indoor pool where we're forced to learn to swim as Coach Powell blows a whistle and yells at us to kick our feet. In kickball, the pitcher rolls the big red rubber ball toward the plate where I stand and go running towards it and kick, missing it entirely and getting the breath knocked out of me when I land on my back. Everything I'm told to do, I'm no good at doing. Can't bridle or saddle a horse or even get my foot in the stirrup. Slide off. Get bucked off. I strike out every time at bat during softball practice. I've never worn a baseball glove or been thrown a softball before, so I'm terrible at catching and throwing. Guys in the dorm are brutal. They ask, "Didn't you have a family that was supposed to teach you this stuff? Don't you have any skills?" I try to think of what my family taught me, what skills I have. Nothing comes to mind. My only expertise is in cartoons.

Two weeks after I get there, Mr. Price makes everybody assemble in the Big Room where we look at a little black kid and his suitcase standing in front of the fireplace. Mr. Price tells us his name is Raymond Hill. He's from Port Arthur, Texas. He's going into the fourth grade, same as me. He's the new guy.

Right away he gets the nickname Razzberry. It sticks. He's made to go to swimming lessons with me, and just about everything else. He tells me that before he got sent here, he was being whipped day and night by mean foster parents. He says he has no memory of any mother or father, only a series of foster homes with the final one being the worst. There were five foster kids there already, every one of them sad and miserable. The husband came home from work every day, got rip-roaring drunk, yelled at the wife, and whipped them all.

After he complained enough, he says Mrs. Barry, his caseworker from the Texas Department of Family and Protective Services, contacted Cal Farley's Boys Ranch to see if they would take him. Mr. Sarpalius from Boys Ranch came with Mrs. Barry to the hell house one day, and he sat Razzberry down at the kitchen table and showed him the same brochures my mother had shown me. He told him about horseback riding and camping, about fishing in the lakes, about playing softball and basketball and swimming in the big indoor pool. He brought out a map of Texas and pointed out Port Arthur down on the gulf and said to him, "You live down here." He moved his finger up to the middle of the panhandle. "How would you like to move up here and go to Boys Ranch?"

"When he asked that," Razzberry says, "all I could say was, how soon can I go?"

At 5:30 in the morning, Mr. Price turns on the lights in Anderson
Dorm. Starting at Room Six, he knocks on the wooden bunk beds
and calls out, "Rise and shine," and works his way down the long
hallway to Room One. It's the same way he wakes us up every
day. I stay in my top bunk bed in Room Two until the last possible
moment, when Mr. Price is right there eyeballing me face to face.
"Rise and shine," he says and knocks on the bed with his big ring.
I like to make a goofy face at him, see if he'll smile. He winked at
me the other day and that made me happy.

I get out of bed and go to my locker. Put on my clothes and my
boots. Take my toothbrush and toothpaste and go to the bathroom,
where eight jerks are already hogging the sinks. Johnny Sagnimeni
tells me to pull his finger. I have to or he'll hit me, so I pull his
finger and he cuts the cheese. It's his superpower. He can fart on
demand at any time, day or night. I think he only uses his powers
on kids like me though.

I have to take out the trash, which I hate doing. The trash barrels
are behind the dorm, way back where the grass stops and the rocky
desert starts, in the pitch black. It's scary. I'm a little bit afraid of
the dark. I've been hearing things moving around in the unseen
darkness when I get close to the barrels, coyotes maybe, or worse,
George of the Water Tower.

Everybody tells me the same thing, so I don't think they're
making it up about George of the Water Tower. They say that years
ago he was painting the letters on the water tower and fell, and in
the process got his hand cut off so now he has a hook. He lives in
the junkyard about a mile and a half behind Anderson Dorm, in an
abandoned school bus that sticks out of a mountain of trash. He
steals from the crops in the field and raids Boys Ranch at night,

especially going after unsuspecting new boys and little boys who are never seen again.

I take the trash bag from my room and go out the door at the end of the hall. The stars are out. The trash barrels are barely visible on the edge of darkness. My ears go into radar mode as I listen for danger. Walking across the lawn toward the barrels, I sing in a low voice "Jesus loves me, this I know." I get halfway there. Something is rustling in the bushes. My heart beats out of my chest. It feels like something is fixing to happen. I get closer to the trash barrels and sing louder. "Little ones to him belong. They are weak but he is strong. Yes, Jesus loves me." I throw my trash bag toward the barrels but miss. It hits the pavement and splits open. I run screaming back to the dorm.

After breakfast, Donnie Winters and I sweep the sidewalks in front of the dorm. Mr. Price has warned me about Donnie Winters, not to be like him because he's a troublemaker always on restriction for some transgression. He missed two haircut appointments in a row, so Mr. Price has given him a buzz cut, bald except for his bangs, which are now kind of like a moustache on the top of the forehead. The big kids call him Donita Bangs. He wants to know what I did that got me sent to Boys Ranch. I tell him I didn't do anything. He says that if I'm not a problem child or an orphan, then the only other reason I was sent here is because nobody wanted me. He says I shouldn't feel bad. Lots of kids here have been kicked out of their families because nobody wanted them.

This couldn't be true in my case. My Aunt Bettye would take me in, she would want me. My Aunt Hedy, my Aunt Payo, Aunt Dottie, all the aunts would let me live with them. So would Uncle Jerry and so would Uncle Lisle, who got a purple heart for serving in World War II. They love me. They would let me stay with them. And Nana, my grandmother, there's no way she would let this happen to me. Something must be wrong. They must not know where I got sent, that I'm here.

But what if I was a bad kid? So bad I got sent here on purpose. All that stuff in the first grade. Like when I got up in the middle of the night and ate chocolate cake with my hands and lied about it and got caught because of all the chocolate on my sheets and on my face and under my fingernails. Then the second and third grades, all the bad things I did, more than just stealing that quarter. Seems like all I ever did at home was stand with my nose in a corner because my mother was mad at me for something. Go put your nose in the corner. That's what she said to me the most. Go pick a switch. That probably came in second. Maybe nobody wants me anymore, not even the family. They probably know I'm at Boys Ranch where I belong with all the other bad boys. Donita Bangs could be right.

Later in the morning when all my chores are finished, Mr. Price finds me sitting alone on the ground behind the dorm. I've been watching an ant, seeing where it goes. "What you doing, Runt?" That's his name for me because I'm the littlest.

"Nothing. Sitting here."

"Why you so down?"

"Oh, nothing."

He finds a key on a crowded keychain and opens the door to a little storage room. "I've been seeing you moping around," he says. "Don't look too happy." He gets me to talking. I get emotional and ask if I can call my mother on the phone and see if I can go home. If only I could talk to her and ask for a second chance because it's not fair. I really don't belong here. I just need to call my mom.

Please, sir, please.

He looks down at me and says, "If you stop your crying, I can talk to you."

I wipe my eyes and nose with my shirt. "Yes, sir."

"Here, help me with this." I stand. He hands me a spool of fishing line and has me stick my fingers in the holes of the spool on the sides so he can wind the string on a fishing reel. When the spool spins around my fingers and the string goes into the reel, he winks and says I'm doing good. "You want to go home, that right?"

"Yes, sir."

"Don't feel like you belong here, huh."

"No, sir."

"I know just how you feel."

"You do?"

"Sure do. Know who else knows that feeling?"

"No."

"About every one of the three hundred boys out here right now." I sniffle some more and look up at him. "Yeah," he says, nodding. "And all them that came here years ago, too. You know who else?"

"Who?"

"Boys and girls all over the world, all the ones that ever lived." My eyebrows go up and get angled in the middle. He explains as he winds the reel and I hold the spool. "You see, Runt, when kids are little, before they go to school, they're kind of like in a sort of bubble of happiness, you know, everybody making goo goo eyes at them, tickling them, giving them presents, making them feel safe and secure, and loved. Innocent, you know?"

"Uh huh."

"It's a shock when something happens. People think, why me?

That's the wrong kind of thinking. Bad things are going to happen. No matter what. Happens to everybody one way or another. All we can do is try to find a silver lining, something good that might come from it. You know?"

"I guess." The reel is full of string now. He threads the string up through the rod's eyelets and hands me the end to hold. "Know how to tie a fisherman's knot?"

"I don't think so."

He takes a hook and shows me how, then tells me to skedaddle. Razzberry and I go play dodgeball at the gym that afternoon with a bunch of guys from other dorms. Mr. Price says it will be fun. We get there. Two captains pick teams. I am the last one chosen. As soon as the game starts, I get hit hard on the side of the head. They scream at me, "You're out!" and make me go stand on the sidelines. It's pure carnage. The little kids stand at the back against the wall as the big kids prowl back and forth along the center line and pick out victims. They throw the ball as hard as they can. There's a lot of screaming and humiliation.

When the game is over, Razzberry and I are relieved and go to walk out. "Where are you going?" they want to know.

I tell them, "Back to the dorm."

"Oh no you're not. You're not allowed to leave for two more hours. The game starts over. Get out here."

Oh my God.

We go out onto the dodgeball floor. The other team has no sportsmanship whatsoever. They yell at us that they're going to kill us. That we're dead. We're dead meat. They say they're going to flatten our faces and that we need to get ready to die. The game starts. It's panic and fear. I run. I dodge. I duck. When I do grab a ball and throw it at the enemy, they laugh. They tell me that I suck and then hit me in the face or in the back and I go stand with the losers on the sidelines. Over and over. Never again am I going to sign up for this shit, that's for sure.

After supper, a bunch of guys at the dorm play a game of tackle the man with the ball. Whoever has the football runs and either throws it or gets tackled and is usually dog-piled. I don't feel like playing. I've already had my torture for today. I sit out front with Donita Bangs's View-Master and take out the reel to see what it is. *Bambi.* The heartwarming story of a fawn, his exciting forest adventures and his curious animal friends. Good gravy. I've seen this one a million times.

Mr. Price's pickup truck pulls up and he calls out through his open window, "Runt, come here." He doesn't get out. All the kids in the yard stop what they're doing and watch. I walk toward the truck, gripped by white-hot fear. What did I do wrong? I try to think. Maybe he's figured out that all that trash blowing in the wind by the trash barrels is because of me.

I go to his window. "Yes, sir?"

He tilts his cowboy hat back on his head and takes a look at me. "Runt, I got something for you. Something that'll help you get over being all homesick. Take a look at what I got here." He motions toward the passenger-side floorboard.

It's a cardboard box. I get up on my tippy toes to get a better look. It's a puppy. I look at Mr. Price and he looks at me. He nods and says, "Come around here and get him."

I go around and look down at the puppy. He's the cutest thing I've ever seen. His bottom teeth stick out like Dick Dastardly's dog, Muttley, from *Wacky Races*. A wave of happiness crashes over me and I burst into tears and crawl up into the truck and give Mr. Price a hug.

"About the best thing for a boy is a dog," he says.

"Is he mine?"

"Yep. Are you gonna take care of him?"

"Yes, sir." When I pick up the puppy, his tail beats fast and he licks my face.

"Does he have a name?"

He exhales and looks none too thrilled about answering me. "Yeah," he says, "I'm not too fond of it, so you can change it if you want to. He's probably too little to really know his name. So you can change it."

"But what's his name?"

"Zappa."

"Oh, I like that name."

Chapter Two

I have two Hot Wheels cars: a Cockney Cab and a Heavy Chevy. Razzberry has four that he won in a bet the other day off of some dude in Edwards Dorm. He's always going on about his Porsche 917 with a rear-opening hood. Pish posh, I say.

We are behind our dorm where the hill is almost vertical, using spoons to carve out roadways on the side of the cliff for our Hot Wheels. He goes to dig a road out right below one of mine. I tell him that if it weakens my road and makes it collapse, he has to give me his Boss Hoss Silver Special. He says no way.

Mr. Price pulls up over by the bicycle racks in his pickup. We go over to see what he's doing. He unloads a bicycle from the back, one with no chain and just metal rims, no tires. He says I can have it, but I have to save up my table-waiting money to get everything it needs.

When Mr. Price leaves, Razzberry tells me he has an idea. He takes the bicycle and carries it through the rose garden behind the dorm. He wants to take it up on the hill, so I carry the back rim and he carries the front. We go up a pretty steep trail between two hills to the top. Zappa goes with us. The idea, he says when we get up there, is to ride this bicycle, that's just rims and that has no chain or brake, all the way down the narrow trail bordered by rocks, cacti, and thorny mesquite bushes, down to the rose garden.

I tell him if I do it, he has to do it also. He says okay. I make him swear. He swears.

Anderson Dorm is up on a hill. We're above that, and you can see just about all of Boys Ranch from up here. You can look out and see the water tower, the valley and the big field below and the dorms around the side, and further on you can see Restriction Hill, the gym, the track, the high school, and the buildings down in Boys Ranch proper—and if you look way out you can see the dry Canadian River bed and the barren emptiness of the Texas Panhandle beyond.

I get on the bike. Razzberry cups his hands around his mouth and addresses the nonexistent audience. "Ladies and gentlemen, Evel Knievel looks ready to attempt this death-defying stunt. Are you sure you want to do this?" He holds an invisible microphone to my mouth.

"Not really."

"He says yes, ladies and gentlemen!"

I push off. The first five to ten feet go fine. Then I hit bumps and rocks and careen side to side like I'm hitting pinball bumpers, going downhill faster and faster. I turn to miss a cactus and then swerve to miss a rock, but I lose control and topple over, hurtling end over end through mesquite bushes and cactus, me going one way and the bicycle going the other. I tumble down into a rose bush. Thorns stick in my back and my arms. I have a mouth full of dirt. My elbow is bleeding.

Now Razzberry rides the bike down and into a total disaster of a crash that is satisfying to watch. He has cactus spines on the side of his face and makes groaning noises on the ground. When he gets up, he tells me that we should get other people to do this. He says we'll call it the Blue Max Club and that riding the skeleton bike down the hill into the rose garden will be how they get initiated into the club.

We go looking for recruits. The easiest ones are the new guys who we tell that being in the Blue Max Club is the best thing they can do to protect themselves from George of the Water Tower. He will leave you alone if you are in the Blue Max Club, we tell them. They ask why. We think fast. Because George of the Water Tower was the original founding father of the Blue Max Club. Right away we get Tony Kennedy, a new guy in the dorm, interested. He's freakishly tall, all skin and bones, like Ichabod Crane with photo-gray glasses. When he goes down the hill on the bicycle, with his elbows and knees making right angles of his arms and legs, he miscalculates and ends up in a spectacular vortex of body parts and a cloud of dust. At the top of the hill, Razzberry and I laugh and point at him. He gets up, spits dirt out of his mouth, straightens his glasses, musters whatever dignity he has left, and walks ramrod straight into the dorm.

The glory of the Blue Max Club is short-lived. One day Mr. Price hears one of the major wipeouts and the bike hitting the back of the dorm and us hooting and hollering. He comes around to see what's going on. He sees the damage we've done to the bike. Spokes are broken and sticking out. The front rim is twisted. The back one is deformed. We stand frozen as he wordlessly looks at us, his mouth half open. He looks down at our new recruit, some bozo from Willis Dorm who looks like he just got blown up by a grenade. The kid tells him about me and Razzberry's Blue Max Club.

"You peckerwoods," he says. "Whose idea was it?"

"Mine," we both say at the same time.

"You're on restriction. Both of you. You're lucky I don't bust your butts."

We say, "Yes, sir. Sorry, sir."

For some reason, I stand at attention and salute him. He just looks at me and shakes his head and walks away. He calls back, "Runt, put that bike in the back of my truck. It ain't yours no more."

Well, that sucks, losing the bike and being on restriction, even though we deserve it. Razzberry and I have to work while everybody else does activities like fishing and riding horseback. At least being on restriction beats having to play dodgeball. That's just abuse.

But we still have to do rodeo practice, which is worse than dodgeball could ever be. It's every Thursday in the summertime, after supper. Thursday mornings I wake up and wrestle with whether I should fake being sick or not, and what kind of sickness could I pull off, realistically. It's hard to fool Nurse Vandergriff at the infirmary. Almost every single kid who goes to see her has to get an enema up the butt, from what I've heard.

Everybody goes down to the rodeo grounds. The little boys riding junior calves go first and then those riding the senior calves go, then steers, then junior bulls, senior bulls, and broncs. Me and the other eight- and nine-year-olds go back behind the chutes to the spur shack and get spurs. We strap them around our boots. We sit on a bench and wait. Every one of us looks grim and on the verge of tears. We just know we're going to be stepped on or get hooved in the face, or get our teeth knocked out, or have to go to the hospital. It's a circus of death.

The men get up on the plank that runs along behind the chutes. A gate opens and cattle run in with the men yelling "Yah, yah, yah!" Now the interior gates close and confine the cows to their chutes. Big boys bring over ropes and pass them up to the men.

I hear Mr. Price in chute two call out, "Runt! Come on."

I always feel like I'm having a heart attack when I get called. I think, maybe if I shit my pants. There's no way they would let me ride rodeo if I shit my pants. Oh, forget it. I go to the chute. Mr. Price reaches down and lifts me up by my belt. He pulls me up into the air and sets me down on the plank. I look at the cow in the chute below.

He says, "Okay, here we go." He gets me by the belt again and lowers me down onto the cow. It moves under me, causing a ruckus. He has to hold me up for a few seconds until it calms down and he puts me back on. I put my hand under the rope, and it gets cinched up tight.

In the next chute, the gate-puller yanks it open and out rockets some poor kid to his doom.

"Scoot up," Mr. Price tells me. "Get up on his shoulders. Get right up on that rope."

I do what he says. The calf moves under me. I can see the gate-puller looking at me through the slats.

Mr. Price still has me by the belt. He says, "Hang on for eight seconds, Runt! You can do it. Let him know when you're ready."

I lean forward and make eye contact with the gate-puller through the slats. I nod. The man slams open the gate. It's off to the races. The cow takes off bucking and turning and twisting. I fly off and land in the dirt. Nobody claps. Ashamed, I run out of the arena. I go back to the shack and say, "Here's your stupid spurs!" and throw them down on the table at the kid sitting there having to put them away.

Technically, Razzberry hasn't been here long enough to go on our summer trip, but Mr. Price lets him come with us anyway. We're near the front of a yellow school bus with Cal Farley's Boys Ranch emblazoned on the sides, headed to Red River, New Mexico. I heard the dorm got to go to Six Flags in Dallas one year, where I'd rather be going because I could run away from there and make it to my Aunt Frances's house. I could hide in her attic like Anne Frank. Running away from Boys Ranch would be a lot tougher. Donita Bangs shot down my ideas about that. Only way possible would be if I hopped a train, but he says I'm way too small to get up on the boxcars and probably couldn't run fast enough anyway. I'd fall and get my legs cut off by the train.

The big boys sit in the back of the bus, followed by normal guys in the middle, progressing up through the geeks and dorks to the front where the little kids like me and Razzberry are. Mrs. Price sits in the very front seat behind Mr. Price, the driver, looking cool with his trademark cop sunglasses.

A slice of an orange splats against the back of my neck. It's the second time I've been hit by an orange in two minutes. I turn and look for the culprit. There's Razzberry, two seats back, looking out a window with a wavering secret smile about to overtake his face. He's the one who threw it, I just know, so I gather up the two slices. Guys in the seat across from me are singing "Great Green Gobs of Greasy Grimy Gopher Guts." Nobody's paying attention. I make a quick throw and hit Razzberry in the side of the head. He's lightning fast and returns fire, but I duck and the slice of the orange sails over me.

It catches Mr. Price's attention. He says, "Next one of you throws an orange is going to get his butt busted." He reaches up and adjusts the big rear-view mirror. Mrs. Price turns to look at us. I put on the face of an angel, but as soon as she turns back around, I give Razzberry a haughty look and silently mouth "ha ha" at him. For good measure, when I face front, I scratch the back of my neck with my middle finger. After a while, the guys in the seat across from me start up with "On Top of Spaghetti" and sing about the poor meatball they lost when somebody sneezed.

A slice of an orange hits me in the back of the head. The bus brakes hard and lurches to the right. Mr. Price shouts, "I told you!" Everybody bounces around as the bus hits bumps on the shoulder. It comes to an abrupt halt that throws us forward. Mr. Price marches past me. He gets Razzberry by the arm and ushers him off the bus.

Razzberry wails and says, "I'm sorry, sir! I'm sorry, sir!" over and over.

All the boys rush to the windows. Mr. Price pulls his belt out from the loops. "Grab your ankles, Razzberry."

"No, please! Please, sir. I won't do it again."

"I know you won't. Now grab them ankles."

Razzberry has a meltdown that goes on and on until he's quaking and quivering and bending over, slowly reaching for his ankles. Mr. Price swings the belt. I pull my head down from the window. Can't watch. Can't take hearing Razzberry scream and cry. He gets three licks, that's all, but it's the first licks he's gotten since he came to Boys Ranch. The rest of the way to Red River, Razzberry sits silently with a sad face that makes me feel awful.

When we get to the campsite in the mountains beside the river and set up our tents, I tell Razzberry I wish I hadn't thrown the orange back at him and gotten him in trouble. To make him feel better, I tell him about when I got licks from Mr. Price, only three days after I got to Boys Ranch. I was in the dugout, being the bat boy, when Anderson Dorm was playing a softball game. Well, Mr. Price's son, Jeff, who's a whole lot bigger than me, kept getting behind me and taking me by both ears and pretending I was an airplane with him doing the piloting and shooting a machine gun with my head. I called him an SOB, which I'd heard someone say the day before. I thought it had to do with a kid who's sobbing all the time, a crybaby.

"What does it mean?" Razzberry asks me.

"It means son of a bitch."

"What's that?"

"A kid born to a mother who wasn't married to the father."

"I thought that was a bastard."

"Oh. Okay, anyway bitch is a bad word for a mom. The SOB is her son."

"How many licks did Price give you?"

I lie and say five, even though it was only three. After I help Razzberry get his tent erected he says, "Thanks, you SOB."

"Why, you SOB." I chase him around.

Anderson Dorm's three table waiters are me, Razzberry, and Donita Bangs, who is back to being called Donnie on account of his hair going back to normal. He gets really sore and will fight you if you call him Donita, so we don't call him that anymore, to his face.

It's a long walk from the dorm to the dining hall where we do our table waiting. We go there and back three times a day, the three of us. Razzberry instigates things. He challenges us to dares. Calls sudden races, like from here to that tree. He gets us to launch snowball attacks on other table waiters walking along with us. He makes fun of them and their dorms. We get chased and get our arms twisted behind our backs sometimes. We've made enemies.

We have to get to the dining hall early so we have time to eat and set our tables with silverware and plates and also to bring out all the bowls of food and bread and the milk and tea and everything. Then hundreds of people show up. When the meals are over, we clean up the tables and take everything to the dishwashing station in the back and sweep and mop the floors.

On the day after Thanksgiving, everything is different. We have to stay late and decorate the dining hall. Some of us put up the Christmas tree on the stage at the front. Some put cardboard Santa Clauses and snowmen on the windows and hang silver garland over the doorways. Some of us take Christmas cards that the ranch has been sent from donors and well-wishers and alumni and tape them to the walls around the insides of the dining hall. There are hundreds of Christmas cards. I love looking at them.

One of the table waiters tells me the greatest rumor ever. He says they let the boys go home for Christmas. We get taken to Amarillo to the bus station or the airport and we get to go home for an entire week. I explode with happiness. I go around and ask. Everybody tells me yes, boys get to go home for Christmas.

I've got a huge spring in my step and I'm singing and dancing in the dining hall with brooms and mops. Getting to go see my mom and my sisters, and my Nana, and all my aunts and uncles and cousins! I can't wait. The whole family will get together and we'll have Christmas in the East Texas woods and sit around the fire and sleep in sleeping bags on the floor and tell jokes all night long. I'll tell everybody what I've had to go through and beg them to let me stay with them. There's no way they will send me back when I tell them the horror.

At the ranch we sing Christmas songs during church service. "Joy to the World." "The First Noel." No Santa Claus or Frosty or Rudolph songs; we have to sing those songs on our own time. I like Christmas songs. I'm good at singing. I'm a soprano. It's probably true that I can sing higher than anybody else at the ranch except Mrs. Price.

We decorate the dorm and put up the tree in the Big Room beside the fireplace and hang Christmas lights along the roof. The dorms have a competition every year for their yard decorations and there's a judge and awards for first, second, and third prizes. This year ours is going to be the Twelve Days of Christmas, painted on plywood boards that are mounted on a rotating metal frame that Mr. Price is going to hook a motor up to. Plus, the lights on our roof are all blue. It makes us look cold and mysterious, I think. Down the road, Edwards Dorm is making some kind of stone house for a *Flintstones* Christmas display. Then there's the dorm that has the baby Jesus in a manger. Boring. Further down, another dorm has a Santa and reindeer on the roof, that's it. Hey, put some effort into it why don't you? We're trying to be jolly.

In December, we get to go to town so we can go Christmas shopping. We're allowed to draw out five dollars from our checking account to buy gifts to wrap and put under the Christmas tree in the Big Room. When we have our Christmas party, we'll draw numbers and get the gifts with that number on it or be able to swap. The less we spend on the gift we have to buy when we get to town, the more we'll have out of our five dollars to spend on ourselves, so we shop wisely at Western Plaza Mall. I could buy someone that Operation game, which looks fun to play on the commercial, but that's $3.66. I could get an Etch A Sketch for $2.83. What's this? A Frisbee for $.94? I buy the Frisbee. That'll be good enough for whatever clodhopper gets it. I have four dollars left to spend on candy and comic books and Hot Wheels for myself. I am rich.

For days I stand around the Christmas tree in the Big Room and look at the lights and the ornaments, the tinsel, the garland, the presents under the tree, the star on top. It's so beautiful. When the Christmas party happens, I draw a number for a present and rip open the wrapping paper to find two crappy comic books: *Korak, Son of Tarzan* and *Timmy the Timid Ghost*. Give me a break. Razzberry picks a number and unwraps his gift. It's the Frisbee I bought. He accidentally throws it into the lake the next day. It sinks. There goes ninety-four cents down the drain.

Everybody in the dorm gets out their suitcases and puts them on their bunk beds and starts packing them with clothes, except for people like Razzberry, who isn't going to get to go home, because he has no home. No mother, no father. A couple of other guys also have to stay for Christmas, I've heard. I get out my suitcase and pick out my best shirts to put in there, socks that go together and underwear that looks not that, shall we say, damaged, and whatnot.

They say that some guys are leaving on Friday and some are leaving Saturday, so I go ask Mr. Price what day I'm supposed to leave. He says he thought I knew. I'm staying at the ranch for Christmas. My mom said so.

I don't get to go home this year.

It takes a while for it to sink in as I go back to my room

shell-shocked and sit and watch the other guys pack their suitcases. Johnny Sagnimeni tells me to pull his finger. I say no, I'm not going to. What's the matter, he wants to know. I don't get to go home, I tell him. He frowns and says, "I'm sorry, little dude."

I put on my coat and go outside and cuddle Zappa on the sidewalk. He can tell something is the matter and starts licking me. We might as well run away and go join George of the Water Tower in the junkyard. Except it's dark already and too scary and there is no George of the Water Tower anyway. Just like there is no Santa Claus. I'm not taking the blame for believing in Santa Claus either. Why should I feel guilty? All my aunts and uncles and my mom and everybody made a big deal about Santa Claus. Telling me I have to be good. That he's looking at everything I'm doing. All the songs. The TV shows. Leaving him snacks. The news saying they've spotted his sleigh on radar. What a crock. So don't look at me like I'm the idiot.

What a crappy Christmas.

When all the lucky ones go home, out into the free world, the thirty-something people in the dorm dwindle down to just me and Razzberry and a few others, along with Mr. and Mrs. Price and their two kids; Jeff, who is a year older than me; Jenny, who is a year or two younger; and our alternate dorm parent, Mr. Weddle, and his family. We remain.

After a period of moping and sitting alone with Zappa out in the cold behind the dorm, I start trying to feel glad everybody else is gone. The few of us left get some perks. Mr. Price lets us watch TV just about any time we want. We watch *Laugh In* and *Maude* and *Carol Burnett*. We watch *Flip Wilson* and cartoons. We run up and down the hall in our socks and slide on the slick floors, chasing one another, especially me and Razzberry. We're like *Spy vs. Spy* in *Mad* magazine. We wad up socks and throw them at each other, aiming for the nuts. We hide behind doorways and when an unsuspecting victim goes by, we hit him in the nuts with a poke of a fist. Everybody gets hit in the nuts so we guard our nuts with our hands and are always on alert when we walk around the dorm. Mr. Price lets us stay up late. He has no idea we are hitting each other in the nuts, or he would make us stop.

We eat some meals at the dorm in the Prices' kitchen instead of going to the dining hall. They let us drink coffee. We hang out in their living room by their tree like we're part of their family. I put on my red pajamas with the feet sown into the pants and stuff a basketball under my shirt and put on a beard and go in their apartment like I'm Santa Claus going "Ho Ho Ho." Anytime Mrs. Price is cooking in her kitchen, we go in and she lets me and Razzberry taste whatever is on the stove and lets us sit at their table. We build snow forts and have snowball wars and come into the dorm to the Big Room to warm up where Mr. Price always has a roaring fire in the fireplace and a bed of glowing coals.

One morning, Mr. Price gets me and Razzberry up earlier, at around 4:30 in the morning, and we get in his truck with him and go to the farrowing barn, where we get to feed little piglets with a bottle. We go to the dairy barn and he shows us how to milk cows and lets us try. We are no good. Another morning, Mr. Price tells us to go down to the horse barn and saddle up horses. We're going hunting and camping on the Canadian River in the snow. He's going to show us how to shoot guns.

We get to the barn and get ropes and bridles on our horses and Mr. Price comes over and helps us put on our saddles because we're too little. He gets me and Razzberry up on our horses. Cameron, a dude from our dorm, gets on his horse. Marvin Perkins and Bob Glawson, other dudes from our dorm, get on their horses and Jeff and Jenny get on theirs. We head out. The snow starts coming down again in big flakes. We go several miles over to the far side of the ranch, past frozen fields, past the railroad trestle, on past Cheyenne, the ghost town that mostly washed away in a flood back in the Old West, to the spot on the Canadian River that Mr. Price told us to head toward.

The snow stops as we make it to the camp where Mr. Price and Mr. Weddle have pulled up in their trucks and are unloading supplies and equipment. We go to the river and tie our horses to nearby mesquite bushes. We find big rocks and slam them down on the ice to punch holes so the horses can drink. Mr. Price lets us shoot rifles. He teaches us how to aim, how to handle the recoil.

We follow Mr. Price's instructions and set up camp. First we fix ropes that go around four trees that he picked out that make a big square. Then we hang heavy woolen blankets on the four ropes and weight the bottoms down with rocks so we're protected from the wind. In the middle, Mr. Price has us make a fire pit with big, flat rocks that we go find by the river. We gather firewood and when the fire gets going we all stand around it warming one side of our bodies, then the other. Marvin says he's not sleeping by the fire in sleeping bags like the rest of us. He's going to build himself a shelter over by a fallen tree. Every so often we check on his efforts and remind him that if he starts freezing in the middle of the night and tries to come over by our fire, he won't be allowed, so he better do a good job. He doesn't. It's beyond shitty and he finally appears out of the darkness to face the music. We let him by the fire in spite of what we said. We help Mr. Price and Mr. Weddle cook supper and then sit around the fire telling jokes and cutting farts and singing songs. Razzberry dances in the fire light and makes us laugh.

On Christmas Eve, we sit on the floor in the dorm by the Christmas tree and watch Sonny and Cher. Razzberry makes fun of Cher when she sings "O Holy Night." He stands by the TV and sings O Holy Crap, but not too loud so Mr. and Mrs. Price don't hear. Then Sonny sings "God Rest Ye Merry Gentlemen" and we just turn it off and run through the dorm hitting each other in the nuts.

Christmas morning comes and there are suddenly many new presents under the tree for the boys, including presents for me from my mom. We rip off the wrapping paper and spend the day playing with all the toys everybody got. Etch A Sketch. Battleship. A four-car racetrack. We are obsessed with an NFL electric football game where you put your players on the field that's made out of metal and stuff a little foam ball into the runner's arm and then turn it on and an electric coil vibrates so that the players start skittering around. Sometimes the runner decides to go sideways, or backwards, or he just spins in a circle. I'm beginning to think the game has no strategy. You surround your runner with your players in a tight ball, turn it on, and hope for the best.

Razzberry and I play Clue and talk about Colonel Mustard in the library with a candlestick. We play pool and accuse one another of not calling their shots. We build a snowman. He wants to make it a snow woman and give it boobs but the boobs keep falling off. We play with the train set he got from Mr. Price. I've never had a happier day in my life.

In the rose garden behind the dorm, the rose bushes are barren and frozen. Razzberry snaps off a dead branch with its thorns. We've been talking about becoming blood brothers and so he stabs his thumb with the thorn from a rose and squeezes it so that a drop of blood comes out. I take the thorn and gouge my thumb. We smash and rub our bleeding thumbs together. Razzberry says that we are now true brothers and always will be.

Then he hits me in the nuts and runs off.

Chapter Three

Istand behind my locker door at the dorm where nobody can see me and smell the envelope and the letter I got from my grandmother. It smells like her and her house and the top of my throat tightens and gets hot when the homesick feeling goes through me. I wish I could run away, but Boys Ranch is so far in the middle of nowhere, it's impossible. They say that a long time ago one kid tried to walk thirty-five miles to Amarillo and died on a barbed wire fence in a blizzard. If I did make it to the free world and went home, my mom would only send me back even if I went to my aunts' or my grandmother's, so I will have to find a new family somewhere who will have me.

Zappa can tell I have the homesick feeling. He never leaves my side. Neither does Razzberry, who also knows something's wrong. I let him read my letters because he never gets any. I tell him about the idea of finding a new family. He says that since he's got nobody, he and I can be a family. We're blood brothers, he says, so we're already a family and we don't need anybody else. Plus there's no escaping Boys Ranch and finding some other family, so we swear to each other that we are our own family. It doesn't matter that he's black and I'm white; no one will ever break us apart. We're all we've got and we're all we need. Me and him and Zappa and that's it.

I think he's right because we're always together, morning, noon, and night, every meal, in school, after school, working, fishing, volleyball, softball, goofing off, Six Flags, Carlsbad Caverns, Palo Duro Canyon, everything. Not in choir though, because Razzberry got kicked off that due to being a bad singer. He also got kicked out of band because he was the worst at playing the tuba Mr. Pimpsell said he ever saw. I watched the disaster unfold. I would be on the alto sax and the band would be playing some simple song and then out of nowhere the loud explosion of Razzberry's tuba would fart on the scene, unwanted, out of time and off key like an ocean liner warning of a collision. Mrs. German, the piano teacher, also told him to go away and never come back, so he doesn't go with me to piano lessons anymore either. He's no good at anything music related, not even dancing, even though he thinks he is. Still, we're together a lot more than people in some families, so we adopt each other.

At the dining hall, I hear people saying that Razzberry had a wipeout on a bicycle and got one of his ankles caught in the back wheel. I hear they took him to the infirmary and that Mr. and Mrs. Price are down there with Doc Calliete and Nurse Vandergriff stitching him up. They say Jeff Price was pedaling and Razzberry was hitching a ride behind Jeff on the banana seat and pretending he was riding a horse and kicking his spurs, telling Jeff and the bicycle horse, "Hiyah! Hiyah!" to get him going faster. He over-pretended and drove his ankle into the spokes. They went end over end in a spectacular wreck.

At the dining hall, a kid on the stage at the front goes up to the microphone and before he says the prayer, he tells everybody that Razzberry was in a serious accident and for us to pray for him.

There's all this sympathy in the loud murmurs and then the kid says the prayer, thanking God for the food and for the hands that prepared it, and for God to please put his healing hands on Razzberry. Dream on, man, I think. I bet Razzberry did this whole thing on purpose. Then I hear he has to stay at the infirmary for over a week. How lucky can he get? Guys in the infirmary get to lie in the bed all day and read comic books and watch TV and get out of work. Here I am sweeping, mopping, buffing floors, going to the dining hall and waiting tables and picking okra and cucumbers and green beans. Hoeing until I get blisters at the elbows of my thumbs. Shoveling manure. Mowing yards. Scrubbing urinals and so forth and so on. I need a break, seriously. Guys in the infirmary get their meals brought to their beds and they sit there and eat their food on trays while they watch TV with a hundred comic books all piled up that you can read any time you like.

I need to get put in the infirmary where Razzberry is. I had to go one time last year for two days and I never wanted to leave. We would have so much fun. I think of ways to fake an illness. A couple of months ago I bet this guy named Britt Hammond in our dorm that I could drink a half a bottle of Listerine. If I could, he had to give me his Bible Trivia Tic-Tac-Toe game. I did it, although I was sick as hell afterwards. And the game wasn't worth it, if you really want to know. Nobody ever wanted to play it except me. Very few people know a lot of trivia about Deuteronomy and Leviticus and second-string characters from the Bible. I got no takers when I paraded the game up and down the hallway.

Listerine. That's the plan. I'll drink some down and throw up in front of everybody. I'll say I have the dire rears, which is what they say people have who shit their pants and can't help it. Also,

Donnie Winters tells me that the magic words are that I feel hot, but then cold, but then hot and then cold. It's foolproof, he says. He's a genius at this sort of thing. He says that as soon as I get to the infirmary they'll take my temperature. If I have a high temperature they will admit me and put me in a bed, so I need to make sure I'm hot. He suggests that if nobody is looking, I should walk fast while holding my breath on the way to the infirmary. I can also drop and do pushups as fast as I can. Better not get caught, he says, because you'll be busted completely. He says I can also take the thermometer out of my mouth if nobody is looking and rub it on my shirt sleeve as fast as I can, but just a little. If I make the temperature go too high, like past 104, they'll bust me and they'll verify the temperature by putting a thermometer up my butt. It's game over at that point.

In the morning, after I drink the Listerine and throw up on the sidewalk, Mr. Price drives me down to the infirmary and takes me to Nurse Vandergriff. We wait out front at the check-in window and then when it's my turn, I tell them I have a dire rear and need to go to the bathroom, and I go there and close the door and do pushups as fast as I can while holding my breath. In the mirror I look hideous, like I just fell out of an airplane. Back at the front, Mr. Price has gone and Nurse Vandergriff puts a thermometer in my mouth. She feels my neck and my arm pits to see if I have any limp nodes. She takes the thermometer out of my mouth and looks at it. And then the glorious moment happens. She hands me a hospital gown and takes me into the ward.

There are five beds on a wall and five beds on the opposite wall. Razzberry and four dudes are on the left, nobody on the right. I'm assigned the middle bed facing all of them. They watch as I change into my gown and put my clothes in a locker. Nurse Vandergriff brings a stainless-steel pitcher of water and puts it on my bedside table as I crawl up into the bed. Razzberry and the four guys stare at me as if they know my secret, but I'm not about to admit to anything because one of them could fink on me; not Razzberry, he's my true brother, but the other ones I barely know and can't trust. They're in other dorms and other grades. For the next couple of hours I act sick and shuffle back and forth to the bathroom and complain about having to take so many craps. What sucks is that the five of them are facing me. They have nothing else to look at.

Razzberry's foot is bandaged and he hobbles around on crutches and uses me to do things like get up and change the channel on the TV and go to the shelves at the front and get him stuff to read. All I can find are stacks of useless old *TV Guides*, *TIME* magazines that are boring beyond belief, and *McCall's* magazines that only women would like. Where are the comic books? Razzberry says they are down in the other ward, where they have the kid with the chicken pox. We're not allowed to go near there. With nothing to read, we watch *Gomer Pyle* and *My Three Sons* and *To Tell The Truth*.

They dare me to sneak down the hall and steal comic books from the other ward. Razzberry urges me on, telling the others that he knows I'm brave and that if anybody could do it, I could. He thinks I'm dumb, and I am dumb because I start thinking I have something to prove to the four dudes I hardly know facing me in their beds on the opposite wall. It's like I'm the star of their movie. They need a hero to go get some comic books? Here I am. I get out of my bed in my back-less hospital gown and my underwear and socks, and slink toward the front, where our ward opens up to the hall.

The coast is clear. Nurse Vandergriff's door is closed. I tiptoe down to the other ward and take a peek. The one chicken pox kid is in there, that's it. He looks to be asleep. I sneak in and go sideways to the shelves and grab a handful of comic books from the top of a stack and take off back to my ward.

I should be met with a hero's welcome with the loot I bring back, but these jerks don't care for the particular comic books I happened to grab ahold of. *Black Beauty*. Okay, I can see how they might not like that one. *The Three Musketeers*. *The Last of the Mohicans*. *Archie*. They say everything I brought back is boring. I grabbed some and ran, I tell them. Beggars can't be choosers.

They dogpile me with advice, as if I have all day to dilly dally in the chicken pox ward under threat of Nurse Vandergriff showing up at any moment and wade through the piles of comic books for the ones they want like *The Incredible Hulk* and *Spiderman* and *Batman*. Get real. I did my duty. I'm the one who breathed in the chicken pox.

Ignoring them, I start reading one of the ones they hated, an old and tattered comic book called *Oliver Twist* from Classics Illustrated. It's about a kid who gets orphaned and sent away to a workhouse for boys. I flip to the back to see how it ends. He gets adopted and lives happily ever after in the country. This could be the blueprint that Razzberry and I need. Speaking of needs, there's a whole back page advertising things I need: imitation vomit, X-ray glasses, sea monkeys that have not only a lifetime guarantee but a booklet that tells you how to train them, and what I needed most, an ad for the secret of how to be taller. My God, if I had all this, I would be unstoppable.

The next morning, after Nurse Vandergriff puts thermometers in our mouths and goes back to her office, I take mine out and rub it on the sheets to hike up the temperature.

"Hey, Razz," I call out. "She says when I go to the bathroom again, she wants to see the stool. What stool is she talking about?"

"She wants to look at your turds."

"What?"

The other dudes in their beds laugh and point at me and say I'm stupid.

"Nurses can tell what kind of sickness you have by studying your turds but instead of turds, they use the word stools," Razzberry says, "and by looking at the color of your pee."

"That's sick." I stop rubbing the thermometer and try to read it. "How do you read these things?"

They tell me to tilt it to where I see the red line, but no matter what I do I can't figure out what it's reading. Nurse Vandergriff comes back, so I put it in my mouth. She comes to me first and takes the thermometer and looks at it. She looks down at me and feels my forehead and my face. Razzberry and the four guys have their eyes glued on me.

"Your temperature is 106. Unusual, don't you think?"

I shrug my shoulders.

"Wait right here," she says and marches away. Everybody's eyes are like silver dollars. Razzberry makes a circle with his fingers and pokes his index finger through the hole over and over. Oh God, no. Razzberry is mouthing something. I can't understand it. He does it again. I think he's saying the word rectal.

Nurse Vandergriff comes back and tells me to turn on my side and to not move. It's game over. The whole reason they give us these open back gowns is clear to me now. The humiliation lasts and lasts while everybody stares until she pulls the thermometer out of my butt and reads it. She tells me to get up and get out, and not in a nice way at all. I change out of my gown and put on my regular clothes and when Nurse Vandergriff isn't watching, I place my *Oliver Twist* comic book on Razzberry's bed and whisper to him to smuggle it out and back to the dorm for me.

Mr. Price is going to tan my hide, that's for sure, plus I'll get put on restriction, and so I drag my feet to school and go the long way. I get there during English class and find out that I won the poetry contest and have to go to the front and recite my poem. Oh no. This will be the end of me. Nobody said I would have to read it out loud.

"I'm sorry, Mrs. Whitney, I don't remember it."

She holds up a piece of notebook paper. "Here it is."

Well, crap. I force myself up and slouch to the front, turn to the mob and give a depressing and sad reading of my poem, "One Little Lamb."

One little lamb was gone and lost.
That one little lamb was me.
I was in the storm, scared and tossed,
But the shepherd set me free.
One little lamb was scared and cold
That one little lamb was me.
But the shepherd tells of streets of gold,
Where I'll live eternally.

The class snickers and everybody makes faces like I'm an idiot, especially Michael Orum, a kid who hates me for some reason. He laughs and points at me.

"Shut up," I tell him as I go back to my desk.

"Make me."

"I don't make trash; I burn it."

"Good," he replies. "Start with that poem."

Mrs. Whitney intervenes before I can come up with a retort and says, "That's quite enough," but she's wrong. This isn't over. I've had it with Michael Orum. Last week during PE, he threw a basketball at me when I wasn't looking, on purpose, and it hit me in the face. He lives in Willis Dorm, just down the hill from Anderson, and said to me one time that if he catches Zappa sniffing around down there by Willis, he'll throw Zappa into the lake. In that case, I will be going to the electric chair because if anybody hurts Zappa, I will send them straight to Jesus, who will drop kick them to you know where. The blood pounds in my veins. Swear to God, I am going to find some way to get Michael Orum. That's what's on my mind, revenge, while Mrs. Whitney goes on and on about things nobody will ever care about like prepositions and adverbs and personal pronouns. I'm not here to write the Bible, Mrs. Whitney. I'm here to teach Michael Orum a lesson. One little lamb is fixing to kick somebody in the face.

Lyndal Waldrip, the kid in front of me, hands me a note while Mrs. Whitney erases the chalkboard. I open the note. It's from Michael Orum and says, "Do you want to fight me? Check one." There two possible boxes to check. The word "yes" is written beside both. Michael Orum looks back at me. I nod.

We will fight after school. The news spreads like wildfire.

My close buddies gather around me by the monkey bars at recess. Michael Orum and his lackeys plot their evil scheme over at the swings.

"Hit him in the nuts," Donnie Winters tells me.

"No, knee him in the nuts, then clobber him on the back of the head," Tim Smith advises.

"Throw salt in his eyes," says Pat McVay. "Like what happened to Bruno Sammartino that time."

I turn to him. "What are you talking about?"

"You know Bruno Sammartino, the wrestler, don't you?"

"No."

"Look," Randy Earle says, puffing out his chest. "Why don't you just let me take care of it?"

"No, there's no way. That would be the worst."

Randy shrugs. "Suit yourself."

At the dining hall when lunch starts, Mr. Price sees me waiting tables. "Runt, come here." I am doomed. The tears almost burst out as I approach him, ashamed and sorrowful.

"Looks like you got better," he says as he butters up a slice of bread.

"Uh huh."

He looks up at me. "Don't look much better, do you?"

"Huh?"

"Never mind. As long as you're better. Probably just had a little stomach thing."

Nurse Vandergriff must not have told him yet about what I did. That puts me on the verge of being happy but then I consider that she could tell him at any moment. I look across the hundreds of people in the dining hall and spot her on the far side.

Maybe if I fess up and tell Mr. Price what I did and that I'm sorry, he'll go easier on me. On the other hand, maybe Nurse Vandergriff got all busy and forgot to tell him and might not remember, so if I say something I might just be finking on myself and get in trouble for no reason. Thank God a table is calling out for some tea. I go get them another pitcher and think it through. If I admit anything to Mr. Price, it will be just about the thermometer, not the Listerine.

Plus, I shouldn't tell him now, at lunch, because if I do, I'll be anxious and depressed about having to get licks and I'll be put on restriction later tonight at the dorm and won't be in any condition to fight Michael Orum when school lets out. I need to be raged up when I fight him, not some sad sack putting up his dukes. What I'll do is wait until lunch is over, when everybody gets up from their tables, and watch to see if Nurse Vandergriff makes her way across the dining hall toward Mr. Price or goes out the door to her car.

She goes to her car. The fight is on. I've only been in one fight before in my life. In the second grade, this kid named Cliff accused me of stealing his quarter. I did, but I wasn't going to admit it and so we had to fight. Nobody landed any punches or made physical contact. We just circled each other jabbing our fists into the air and making mean noises.

The whole afternoon, it's impossible for me to pay attention in class as I watch the clock and think what a rotten day this is turning out to be. If only I could run away from this place! Unfortunately, I don't want my legs cut off by the train, I can't steal a horse because I'm too little to bridle it by myself and get up on it, and my feet don't touch the pedals so I can't steal a car. Why won't my mother come and get me? Every letter I write, I beg and beg to go home. I get letters back from her telling me all about my sisters and what they're doing, about their new church in Dallas, about my cousin Perry who came back from Vietnam all messed up but who's accepted Jesus now and is going to church with her and the girls. Well, I accepted Jesus a long time ago, but he's not doing me any good. I've prayed a million times for him to rescue me.

When the final bell rings, I feel like I'm about to throw up. Six or seven kids from class gather around Michael Orum and me near the gymnasium behind big bushes that shield us from teachers and staff.

"You want to fight? Let's fight," he says.

"I'll fight."

"Then let's fight."

"I will."

He comes up to me, his shoulders pulled back, his chin jutting out and says, "You're too much of a goody two-shoes to fight." I push him. He rushes me and we go to scrapping in the bushes. I try to get him in a scissor lock with my legs, but he squirms out of it. We get back up and face off with our dukes up. I dodge the wild punches he throws at my face and deliver a blow to his ribs. He rushes me and tackles me. I fall face first into the side of the building. Blood pours out my nose. It's on my hands and my shirt.

When Michael Orum sees, he says, "Oh God, now we're going get in trouble." The onlookers take off to their dorms. His dorm is in the same direction as mine, so we walk together and I wipe my face with my shirt. "Pinch your nose," he says. "That'll stop the bleeding."

We come up with a story because Mr. Price will see the blood on my clothes even if I can make it inside the dorm and wash up before he sees me. We'll say that I ran around the corner and collided with Michael Orum accidentally and fell and hit the wall. As long as nobody finks on us, this should work. He finally goes his way and I go across the Willis dike and up the hill to the dorm.

Mr. Price, fiddling with a lawnmower, sees me before I make it across the front lawn. I start crying suddenly. "Runt, come here." He stands up from the mower and watches me approach. "Why are you bleeding?" I go into the story. He buys it. "Come on, let's get you cleaned up."

He takes me into the dorm and into his apartment where Mrs.

Price, in her white nurse's uniform, digs in her purse. When I see her, I bust out crying even more because my goose is cooked. I didn't think about the Mrs. Price and Nurse Vandergriff connection.

"What happened?" she asks.

"I fell into a wall."

"Fell into a wall?" She shoots Mr. Price a question with her eyes. He shrugs. She goes and gets a wet washcloth and wipes my face. "What are you crying for? There's no reason to cry."

Oh, but there is. I'm crying for it all now. It's flooding over me, being sent to Boys Ranch, that horrible night on the bus, being forsaken, incarcerated, having a thermometer put up my butt, fixing to get busted and put on restriction, the humiliation of reading that poem, and having to fight, everything. I can't tell them any of that as a reason for crying, though, and so I tell them I want to go home because I'm not good at anything, being so tiny, so short.

"Not good at nothing?" Mr. Price asks.

"No, sir, not really."

"What about a violin? Are you good at playing a violin?"

"No."

"Why not?"

"I never played one."

"Then how do you know you're not good at it?"

I sniffle and look up at him. Mrs. Price says, "I hear you're good on the saxophone. First chair, aren't you?"

"Yes, ma'am."

"Isn't Lester Goins second chair alto sax?"

"Yeah."

"He's what, six feet tall or something already, right? Last year wasn't he Goliath in the church play and you were David?"

"Yes, ma'am."

"I guess him being so big doesn't matter if you're first chair alto sax and he's second chair." She takes me to her kitchen sink and I wash my hands. "Take off that bloody shirt. I'll put it in our wash."

I take off the shirt and give it to her. Mr. Price says, "You might be good at a whole lot of things, you never know. Whatever you really like doing, you keep doing and one day you'll get good at it. Now get going and put on a shirt and get ready for supper."

"Yes, sir."

I scamper off but he calls out before I get out the door. "And Runt, one more thing."

"Yes, sir?"

They both have their chins tucked into their necks and they give me knowing looks over the tops of their eyes. He says, "Nurse Vandergriff wants you to know that next time you go to the infirmary, there's only one way she's checking your temperature from now on."

Oh no. The shame flows over me.

Chapter Four

Anderson Dorm sits on a hill surrounded by three lakes. Whenever we get a chance, Razzberry and I grab our fishing poles, run out of the dorm, and cast out in less than a minute. The guys in the other dorms, being located much farther away from the lakes, can't fish nearly as often. They don't even know what they're doing. We have things in our tackle boxes they can only dream of. Consequently, we have a reputation for being major fishermen. World class. Boys just pass out and have to go to the infirmary because of the awe they feel when people talk about our fishing skills.

The fifth grade is a cutthroat world when it comes to fishing at Boys Ranch. Boys big and little crowd the banks and argue over crossed lines. When lines are crossed, you bring the tangled knot up to the shore and you cut your enemy's line, sending his weight and his hook and his bait to the bottom of the lake as fast as possible and especially if you can do it before he knows you're doing it. You tell him to pack sand and move off from your fishing grounds. It's the same way animals protect their territory on *Mutual of Omaha's Wild Kingdom*.

Two seconds later you move to another spot and repeat the cycle with whichever kid happens to be standing there trying to fish and you threaten him with the warning, "You better not cross my line."

There are a lot of ups and downs and waiting and boredom in fishing. Razzberry and I spend it laughing and singing songs from the radio and acting out scenes and sound effects from *The Six Million Dollar Man,* mostly. It's easy. You run in slow motion and make the dun-nu-nu-nu-nu-nuh sound that the bionic man makes when he runs, and you vary or escalate the pitch of the dun-nu-nu-nu-nu-nuh at random intervals. The most important thing, though, is to intone the words that narrate the beginning of each *Six Million Dollar Man* episode. "Steve Austin, astronaut, a man barely alive. Gentlemen, we can rebuild him. We have the technology."

Razzberry and I know all the good spots to dig for worms, and that if you take the ladder down into the concrete spillway—which isn't allowed—you can harvest leeches from the slimy walls to use for bait. We catch grasshoppers a lot, but I don't think we've ever caught a bass off a grasshopper, only bluegills. We get leftover liver from the dining hall or the slaughterhouse when we want to fish for catfish. When the grasshoppers disappear and we don't have any bait at all, we use little flowers like daisies to catch a bluegill and then use the bluegill's eyes and organs for bait. One time we put just the head of a bluegill on a hook and threw it out and caught a big bass.

Sometimes when we are bored we sit on the concrete slab at Willis Lake and when we catch a small bluegill, we reel it in a little and tighten the line and then with one quick sudden jerk, haul the fish out of the water high into the air and flip it behind us so that it splats on the asphalt road. We award points for the loudest, most hideous and violent landings.

Razzberry taught me how to fish for frogs. Big Morris Lake has large Texas bullfrogs. At night, their deep, groaning croaks are used to guard their territory or attract females. Razzberry taught me that bullfrogs like to sit out on the lake on top of the moss. You can spot one by looking for the two prominent humps over the eyes poking up from the moss. Then you take a plastic worm rigged weedless style and cast out so that it lands beyond the frog, behind him. You reel in the worm across the top of the moss straight at the frog. Sometimes the frog sees it and starts booking across the moss and eats it, and sometimes you have to reel the worm right to the frog's head and twitch it around to get him pissed off. Almost every time, the frog eats the worm and you can reel that sucker in across the top of the moss.

If the frog is big enough and has large, muscular legs, then it's time to get primitive. We knock him out with a conk on the head and cut his legs off, skin them, and take them to Mr. Price, who puts them in the freezer with all the other frog legs and fish the kids in the dorm have been accumulating. Over time, when we get enough frog legs and fish, we have a fish fry for the whole dorm.

Razzberry and I each claim to be the best fisherman. Sometimes he's in the lead and has bragging rights, but then I make a comeback with some miracle catch. He inevitably gets lucky. Back and forth.

I hear Mr. Price talking to people in the dining hall about how Razzberry is such a good fisherman and that just chaps my ass red and raw. Then a day or two later, I sit on the footbridge that goes across Little Morris pond below the Anderson Dorm hill. I don't have any bait and there is nothing in my tackle box except hooks and bobbers and weights. I have two slices of bread that I tear off pieces of and feed to the ducks swimming near the bridge. Something huge comes up from the deep and inhales a chunk of bread floating there, so fast I barely catch a glimpse of it before it disappears. My heart races. I can only think of one thing it can be: the biggest catfish of all time, an impossibly huge world record.

I know what to do. I reach for my fishing pole and replace the single shank hook with a treble hook. I tear off a piece of bread and squeeze it in my hand, kneading it into dough, and then I press the dough ball onto the treble hook and form it securely there. My legs dangling down off the bridge, I make a gentle underhand cast to toss my bait right where I saw the fish.

Time stands still. The giant fish takes the dough ball. The treble hook digs deep into the cartilage on the side of the mouth. My rod bends in half. Yelling, I hang on, my teeth clenched, my face a hideous grimace, my pencil-thin biceps at maximum power as the great fish dives into the depths.

I pull the rod up, but the fish is too strong. I can't turn the handle on the reel to bring him up. My rod bends down even more and the catfish overcomes the drag and takes out line. On the opposite bank, I spot Russell Parker swinging a sling blade to cut tall weeds because he's on restriction and is working on the chain gang. He's fifteen or sixteen. He's huge compared to me. I'm like a hobbit, one of the small ones.

I cry out, "Russell!" and get his attention. He sees me and drops the sling blade and goes into heroic action, sprinting down the bank and over the bridge. He grabs my fishing pole but doesn't wrench it out of my two hands. He just stands over me and helps hold the pole steady and tells me to start reeling. He coaches me and lets me bring it up from the deep and let it tire itself out. I pull it up onto the bridge despite its bulk. Russell watches me carry it up the hill to show Mr. Price and goes back to cutting weeds. Everyone is amazed at the huge catfish. I am the king.

I am only able to strut around with my fame and celebrity for a couple of days before the tide turns. Razzberry is on restriction and is supposed to be pulling weeds in the yard, but he goes over to Big Morris lake where this dude named Cameron is standing on the bank fishing. Cameron spots a huge bass sitting on a spawning bed, but he has no bait and no lures so he's trying to bare-hook it. Razzberry watches and offers Cameron a bunch of unwanted advice and instructions.

The water is crystal clear. Cameron casts his hook so it sinks down to the middle of the bed. The bass swims up from the darkness beyond, hovers directly above the hook, and then BAM! Cameron yanks his rod but misses. The bass swims away. Cameron casts out again and puts the hook in the middle of the bed. The bass comes back and hovers. This time he hooks it in a fin and they start hooting and hollering as he tries to land it, but as he gets it up near the shore, the line breaks and the bass flops around sideways in the moss. Razzberry jumps in the water and tackles it, then he plops down and wraps his arms around it. It nearly slips away a couple of times, but he holds on and gets his thumb into the mouth and raises it up out of the water with a rebel yell.

I'm in the dorm when I get wind of some commotion and people saying something about Razzberry and running outside to see what is going on. Mr. Price and twenty of us stand on the porch and see Razzberry walking up, soaking wet in all his clothes, a smile on his face, holding a huge largemouth bass.

Even though it is against the rules to get in the lake for any reason, especially when you are on restriction and supposed to be working, I see Mr. Price smiling and proud when he hears Razzberry's story,

with Cameron backing him up all the way. Mr. Price takes the
fish by the mouth and holds it up, feels its weight and looks down
at Razzberry, beaming, and everybody breaks out cheering and
chanting, "Razz! Razz! Razz! Razz!"

I endure the constant pitter-patter of his gloating and his dec-
larations of superiority for a long while. But then the sixth grade
fishing tournament arrives. All the boys bring their fishing poles and
tackle boxes to school that day because Mr. Weddell, our geography
teacher, is taking us straight from school to the other lakes across
the ranch over near the horse barn for the tournament, where the
winner gets a banana split and gets their picture in the Boys Ranch
newsletter.

I have never had any luck at those lakes, plus I forgot my tackle
box back at the dorm. Mr. Weddell doesn't let me go get it. All I
have is what's already tied on my fishing pole: a hook and an orange
rubber Mr. Twister worm. I haven't caught anything with it ever,
so I figure I'm screwed.

When we get to the lakes, I walk the perimeter and look out to
see if there are any bass on the spawning beds, because it's that
time of year. I see the other dudes mindlessly casting their lines out
anywhere and everywhere. Walking along, I spot a huge largemouth
bass close to shore on a bed, but I spook it and it swims away only
to return a few minutes later.

I drop the Mr. Twister in the middle of the bed, and here comes
the bass. This is going to be easy, I think. But the bass has no interest
whatsoever in my worm. I twitch the rod to jiggle it around. I cast
and recast, but nothing happens. So I take the worm off because
I'm going to try to bare-hook it when it hovers over the spawning
bed again.

Anytime anybody comes near me, I slap the water with my fishing rod to scare the bass away so that they don't see it. Otherwise, I'd have five assholes crowding me and invading my honey hole. Bare-hooking it doesn't work even though I try and try. I try talking a couple of guys into letting me borrow one of their lures, but there's no way that'll happen, not with a banana split at stake.

Mr. Weddell calls out, "Ten more minutes!" and panic sets in. I go back to my orange Mr. Twister. This time I wait for the bass to swim up to the bed and then cast out and reel it fast across its nose. Wham! He takes the bait, and I yank the pole and set the hook. I pull it on shore and know right then that I just won the tournament. Eight pounds, twenty-four inches long.

I carry it over to Mr. Weddell and everybody standing there with their mouths open and their eyes bugged out. They parade me to the snack counter at the country store down by the Boys Ranch zoo (we had a buffalo, a Texas longhorn, two or three deer, and a rabbit), where I claim my banana split and wolf it down. It's quite shameful the way I spoon shovelfuls into my mouth, but I don't care. I stumble over to where they want to take my picture. I feel bloated and sick.

The rest of the year and through the winter, I can't catch anything. I lose many lures in trees and overhead wires. A thief raids my tackle box. I suspect Razzberry but can't prove it. One day I trip over Razzberry's line and cause a hook to sink into his thumb. He has to go the infirmary and have it cut out by the doctor. Tragically, they blame me, even though it really is my fault.

In the summer of the seventh grade I have another big moment when Anderson Dorm goes on a camping trip. Every year the whole dorm mounts horses and rides off to camp far away at a series of distant lakes near Cheyenne, an abandoned ghost town out past all our huge fields of vegetables. We sleep in sleeping bags on the lake shore, clustered up around a massive campfire, and ride horses on adventures over a three-day weekend.

One of the lakes has a concrete slab along the shore with a tin roof going over it and it is where we set up base camp every year, where the trucks and vans pull up with the cooking stoves and the coolers and supplies and sleeping bags and everything. I claim a spot by the water and put down my sleeping bag and my tackle box. I start catfishing. Most of the other guys ride off to hunt rattlesnakes or go skinny-dipping in the Canadian River or just ride around on horses like maniacs.

I sit on the slab for hours, late into the night, and haul out one after another until I have eight fat and gorgeous channel catfish on two stringers that I tie off to a stump next to my sleeping bag. I lie down around midnight, glowing with the anticipation of the morning when Mr. Price and everybody gets up and sees all the fish I caught. We'll have us a big ol' fish fry, that's for sure.

In the middle of the night, I wake up with my arm in intense pain, white-hot agony. It's impossible not to whine and cry. Kids around me in their sleeping bags tell me to shut up and threaten to kill me. The pain ratchets up. They threaten to throw me in the lake. Mr. Price gets up and comes over with a flashlight. He sees my arm bright red all the way up to my chest and makes me turn my sleeping bag inside out. A dead scorpion comes tumbling out. I must have crushed him in the sleeping bag with all my thrashing about. Mr. Price goes and gets Mrs. Price and they give me ice from the cooler wrapped in a rag to hold on the scorpion bite.

"Nothing else we can do," Mr. Price tells me. "You're going

have to just ride it out, Runt."

So I take the scorpion pain all night. In the morning I am eager to show everybody the massive quantity of huge catfish I've got on the stringers. The whole dorm stands there waiting on breakfast and watches me hobble down to the shoreline. I tell them, "Take a look at this," and pull the stringers up out of the water.

There's nothing but the heads. Damn turtles got them.

Chapter Five

Istand in front of the mirror checking myself out. I have on an orange wide-collar dress shirt. Brown pants. A white belt. White shoes. I comb my hair. Spit on my fingers. Slick my bangs across my forehead. Three other dudes crowd me at the sinks. Razzberry, whose hair goes up instead of down, uses a pick on the little afro he's got going. The radio plays in the next room. I jump in on the chorus to "Billy Don't Be a Hero" and give it all I've got.

We get on the bus parked in front of our dorm and head toward Amarillo, forty miles away. Each dorm gets to go to town every third Saturday. We love it. Amarillo is the Pleasure Island of the Texas Panhandle, where we turn into jackasses, where we play pinball and go to the movies. It's the big city where we buy candy, shoot pool, smoke Swisher Sweets like bankers, and puke on neighborhood sidewalks.

Razzberry wants me to pool my money with him. We each have two dollars and twenty-five cents. We can go bowling, he says. See a movie. Get Dr. Peppers. The main thing, he says, is that we can buy a big bag of Starburst that we share, me and him, back at the ranch. Plus we'll have fifteen cents left over that will go to whichever one of us wins at bowling.

I'm thinking this is going to be an easy fifteen cents. Bowling is my thing. My method is the granny style. I use both hands, the bowling ball between my outstretched legs, and roll it slow and straight up the middle. All these other idiots roll gutter balls, especially Razzberry, who tries to throw it too hard.

When the bus gets to Amarillo at the Boys Ranch town office, we pile out and take off running through Ellwood Park in the direction of the interstate. We always go a certain way through the park to avoid the bathroom building because the rumor is that if you go near the bathrooms you have a 100 percent chance of being molested by perverts. We used to stop in the drugstore and buy candy, but Razzberry got caught stealing a pack of Juicy Fruit last month and we're not allowed to show our faces in there anymore. We take side roads that parallel the interstate, and make our way the three miles to the bowling alley.

We stick our fingers in many bowling balls and feel their weight. At long last we select the perfect ones and go to our lane. Next to us we see three girls our age with a mom and a dad. I fall in love with one of the girls at first sight. She looks like Kristy McNichol.

Razzberry goes first. He knocks down one pin and follows it up with a gutter ball. It's my turn. I decide not to embarrass myself in front of my future wife and abandon my successful granny style method. I roll the ball like a normal person would. It makes such slow progress down the lane that it's on the verge of stopping. It drops off into the gutter and I turn in shame to face the girls, the mom and the dad, and Razzberry, who can barely contain his glee. I lose the game. My soulmate walks out the door with her family as I give Razzberry three nickels.

I want to see *Where the Red Fern Grows* at the movies over

at Western Plaza Mall, but Razzberry doesn't want to spend his money on that. He gives me his half of the money for the bag of Starburst and goes with some other Boys Ranchers to walk around the mall. I go watch the movie about a boy and his coon dogs, how they save him from a mountain lion, how the boy dog dies on the kitchen table and the girl dog loses the will to live. When it shows the red ferns growing on the dogs' graves, I cry hard in the darkness of the theater. I'm alone, thank God. No one can know about this.

That evening I do my duty. I buy a bag of Starburst and keep it unopened as it is supposed to sustain us through three hard weeks at Boys Ranch and Razzberry says we have to split the candy exactly in half. I go with a pack of boys the three miles back to the town office, bypass the bathrooms at Ellwood Park, and get on the bus.

Halfway on the forty-mile ride back to Boys Ranch, Razzberry, who's sitting a couple of seats behind me, comes up and says I should check out Rod Urquidi's new skateboard. He shows it to me. The wheels and the ball bearings are super smooth and quiet, he tells me, handing me Rod's skateboard and offering to hold the bag of Starburst I have in my lap.

So I hand him the bag of Starburst. He goes and takes his seat. The skateboard wheels are fascinating. So quiet and smooth. I settle back and start thinking about the coon dogs in the movie.

We get to Boys Ranch and the bus parks at Anderson Dorm. Mr. Price and Mr. Weddell tell us to go to the Big Room, where we empty our pockets and place everything we brought back from town on the pool table. We strip down to our underwear. It's how they go through everything for contraband like cigarettes, matches, and dirty magazines. I have nothing to declare except the bag of Starburst I'm sharing with Razzberry.

I get in my bunk bed, my brain fixating on scenes from the movie, on Poor Billy and those coon dogs, and that grandpa. Not long after I fall asleep, the beam of a flashlight hits me in the face. Mr. Price looms over me and tells me to get up and go to the Big Room. When I get there, I see Razzberry and go stand by him, the two of us in our whitey tighty underwear. Four men stare at us: Mr. Price, Mr. Weddell, Mr. Simmons, and Mr. Pegram.

Simmons and Pegram are the most-feared staff members at Boys Ranch. They are senior administrators who are summoned by the dorm parents when corporal punishment is to be dished out, to serve as witnesses per various new regulations. Or maybe just for the fear factor, which is working. They stand by the pool table with the bag of Starburst. Simmons, stern and emotionless, is like Yul Brynner in *Westworld*. Pegram, always with a crumpled cowboy hat and chomping on a third of a cigar, walks with a pronounced limp. Thing is, he has a three-legged dog. If you see Simmons and Pegram in their truck headed your way with that dog gimping along gamely trying to keep up, you know somebody is about to get it.

They show us the slit they've found cut in the bottom of the bag. They show us the can of Copenhagen dipping tobacco they say was stuffed inside.

"It's not mine," I tell them, breaking into tears. "I don't know who put it in there! Jesus and God know I'm innocent, I swear! I swear to God. Swear to God."

"Somebody must have put that in there," Razzberry says. "It's not ours!"

"Stop lying," Mr. Price growls.

"I'm not lying!" I say. "Ask Jesus! Jesus knows!"

Mr. Price unlatches his huge Texas belt buckle and pulls his fat leather belt out of the loops. "You two peckerwoods know better," he says to us. "Now bend over and grab your ankles, you first, Runt."

"Please! No! Noooo!" I back up against the trophy case. Simmons grabs me by the neck and maneuvers me toward the middle of the room. Forces my head down. I see Mr. Price get behind me and double his belt. I raise up and shield my butt with my hands. Simmons forces me back down and puts my head between his knees like a vise.

"Move your hands or you'll get more," Mr. Price says. He swings the belt. I scream. It's the worst stinging in the world. All I've got on is my underwear. I squirm to wrench myself free, but Simmons holds me down and squeezes my head between his knees harder.

"Move your hands! Put 'em on your ankles!"

Another lick, worse than the first. I scream and struggle and cry for him to stop. But he doesn't. Another one and another one and another. Simmons lets me up after the tenth lick. I go stand against the wall, convulsing in tears, a blubbery mess.

They start on Razzberry. I can't watch. I squat on my haunches and put my hands over my face. But nothing stops the sounds. The whooshing and the cracking of the belt. The howling and screaming.

They tell us we're on restriction and hard labor for three weeks. I'm reeling, stumbling out of the Big Room down the hall to my room because it doesn't seem possible. How could Mr. Price not believe me? I have never told a lie, as far as anybody knows, and Copenhagen and Skoal and all that stuff is gross. How could I buy it anyway? What kind of person would ever sell it to me?

Why would they not believe me? I gave my testimonial in front of the church a couple of weeks ago. People said it was good. I'm in the Bible Memory Association. I won the Sword of the Lord Bible

Drill last summer. I'm in the choir. I go to Bible camp. I definitely do not dip. That's gross. But all of a sudden I'm being accused of being a criminal and being forcibly bent over and beaten with a belt in my underwear in the middle of the night?

Mr. Price calls us the Salt and Pepper Gang as we are the only two in the dorm currently on restriction. While everybody else fishes and goes hiking, rides horses, goes swimming and everything, Razzberry and I have to work. Sweeping the road. Hauling rocks. Picking okra. Moving irrigation pipes. Slopping pig stalls. Shoveling cow manure. Waxing and buffing floors.

Guys in the dorm laugh at us and poke fun at the idea of us smuggling a can of Copenhagen in a bag of Starburst. Nobody believes our story, that we were framed. They taunt me because I'm such a goody two shoes. Now I'm a dirty rotten scumbag, a tobacco smuggler on the Boys Ranch chain gang getting my comeuppance. Everything is such a drag. No more happy-go-lucky optimism. No more of my joking and wisecracking. I don't say prayers to Jesus at night. What's the use?

Then on the sixth day of the Salt and Pepper Gang when we're pulling weeds in the front yard, Razzberry tells me the Copenhagen was his and that he put it in the bag of Starburst. I've secretly suspected this. He says he wouldn't blame me if I go and tell Mr. Price and that he deserves ten more licks and three more weeks of restriction on top of what he already has. I say no. I'm not going to fink on him. He stands and tells me I'm his true brother.

"Watch this," he says. "I'm going to get you off restriction right now."

"Where you going?"

"I'm telling Price you were innocent." He leaves the pile of weeds he'd been picking and walks into the dorm.

Not long after, I see a truck coming up the road. A dog runs behind, zigging and zagging and trying to keep up. A three-legged dog.

Oh shit. Simmons and Pegram.

I hide when the truck pulls up to the dorm, and then I go in a side door and slink down the hall to get near the Big Room to hear what they're saying. When I hear the crack of Mr. Price's belt hit home and Razzberry cry, I turn and run down the hall and out the door.

Chapter Six

The book I am writing, titled *The Incredible UFO*, is off to a good start with thirty handwritten pages in a spiral notebook. It has lots of drawings, mainly to fatten out the book so I don't have to write so much. I'm aiming for one hundred pages. The story is about a boy living at a different Boys Ranch who finds a UFO in the desert that he commandeers so he can escape. Not only does he escape the Boys Ranch, he flies all over the world and then to other planets, having adventures and saving people. The problem is that I tried to be nice to this new kid in the dorm, David Ralls, and named the main character in *The Incredible UFO* David Ralls. Now I have to go back over all the thirty pages I have written so far and change the character's name to David Rallsmey because David Ralls has pissed me off royally. It will be easier for me to pencil in the extra letters, smaller, crammed in sometimes, than change the whole name. Too bad for him. He lost his chance to be known in literature for being a space adventurer. I guess David Ralls will think twice before he finks on me to Mr. Price about hoarding sugar packets from the dining hall, won't he?

Lately, though, I've had to put my book on the back burner so I can concentrate on the upcoming Boys Ranch Christmas poetry contest. There's no way I'll repeat the mistake of "One Little Lamb," that's for sure. I'm not writing a poem about Jesus in the manger or the wise men or angels or any of that crap. Instead, I sit at the table in Anderson Dorm, Room Two and try to make progress on my poem, "That Fat Old Man In My Living Room."

> Santa Claus they say is just a myth,
> But how odd it was on December twenty-fifth,
> When I woke up in the middle of the night,
> And went downstairs and got a fright.
> There was a gigantic, fat-looking slob,
> And in all his red clothes, he looked like the Blob.
> It's a prowler, I thought, a thief on the loose,
> So I got down my gun from the mouth of my moose.
> Cautiously I moved toward this dude,
> But I couldn't just shoot him, I might get sued.
> So I said, "Stick 'em up. You're caught in the act."
> He said, "Ho, ho, ho, is that a fact?"
> He was dressed like Santa, but I'm no fool.
> He was a robber, disguised, so I kept cool.
> Alright, Mister, I said acting tough.
> I'm calling the cops, but I can get rough.
> One false move and you'll have lead in your bod.
> But I'm Santa Claus said the ignorant clod.

Michael Orum would never make fun of this poem. Besides, he doesn't hate me anymore after our fight last year. I come up with the next lines.

Alright, you klutz, show me your sleigh.

If you're Santa Claus, then I'm Doris Day.

Perfect.

"Runt!" It's Mr. Price. I go to the door of my room and look down the hall. Light streams out from his office.

"Sir?"

"Come here, Runt."

Oh God and Jesus save me. What did I do now? Nobody gets called down to the office unless they're in trouble. What could it be? No idea. I take my poem and put it in my locker beside "The Incredible UFO" and go down the hall. He doesn't look mad, though, sitting behind his desk. He holds a letter in front of him.

"Guess what?"

"What, sir?"

"Got this here letter. From your mom. She says you're going to be going home for Christmas."

"Really?"

"That's right. A whole week back home, how's that?"

I jump and let out a happy scream and dance around like a maniac. I run over and give him a hug, telling him, "Thank you, thank you, thank you!" and bury my head on his shoulder and pat him like I would a cat.

"Thought that would put a spring in your step. She's got you a bus ticket to Dallas and back."

I run down the hall shouting, "Yay!" Razzberry pokes his head out of Room One and wants to know what's going on.

"I'm going home for Christmas!"

I run into my room and fall on the floor on my back, squirming around in a happy ecstasy. Razzberry stands over me saying, "No! Don't you dare! I need you, you SOB." We go to wrestling around on the floor as I laugh and chant, "I'm going home and you're staying here," over and over until he clamps his hand over my mouth and we roll over into some chairs. He's actually happy for me, he says at last and makes me promise to bring him back something from the free world. I say I will, even though I know I probably won't.

Nobody's ever seen a kid with as much Christmas spirit as me. I decorate Room Two with drawings on construction paper of Santa and elves and Christmas trees all the while singing every Christmas song I know, except for "The Little Drummer Boy." For one thing, the song is boring and depressing and for another thing, the Bible doesn't make any mention of some kid glomming onto the three wise men. It says nothing about him going into the manger and banging a drum in the poor baby Jesus's face. I don't think there's any baby in the world, not even baby Jesus, who'd put up with that for two seconds. I only sing that song when I change the words to annoy Razzberry and David Ralls, in which case I sweetly sing, "Come, they told me, oh boy aren't you dumb? A newborn king to see, oh boy aren't you dumb? Dummy dumb dumb."

One of the drawings I taped to the wall doesn't meet with Mr. Price's approval and he makes me take it down and put it in the trash. It was my best one, I thought. I put four pieces of construction paper together so the poster would be big and then I borrowed color markers from Tony Kennedy and took a lot of time drawing a perfect bus with my face sticking out of one of the windows. I drew a big smile on my face and wrote "Ken" on my shirt so there'd be no mistaking who it was. Next, behind the bus, sad in his toboggan cap and winter coat, I drew Razzberry and two snowmen pointing at him and laughing. In big block letters across the top I wrote, "I'll be home for Christmas," surrounded by musical notes. It should have won a prize, but instead it's in the trash barrel. Mr. Price doesn't give me any reason. He just says I should know better.

"The Fat Old Man in My Living Room" is hailed as a masterpiece and Mr. Price tacks it up on the bulletin board beside his office. I recite it during our class party on the last day of school before Christmas vacation. People like the twist at the end when it is revealed that the fat old man in the living room is a robber indeed, just like I thought at the beginning of the poem. David Ralls gets on my good side and so, in the Christmas spirit, I re-change the character's name in *The Incredible UFO* from David Rallsmey back to David Ralls with my eraser. Why not? Jesus has answered my prayer and is letting me go home. Christmas is more magical and holly jolly than ever. Forget Santa, I've got Jesus. He came through. He sat there in the manger, surrounded by animals, having to deal with the incessant drumming of that drummer boy for God knows how long. What were the adults thinking? Strange men? Come on in, watch the manure. We're about to put the baby Jesus to sleep. Oh, that street urchin wants to bang on a drum? Go ahead. Being the son of God, Jesus could have destroyed that kid in one second. I would have, but he didn't because he died for our sins and was able to deal with the drumming. Now he's answered my prayers and is the real reason for Christmas. I get it now.

Mr. Price calls, "Lights out!" and turns off the lights from Room Six down to Room One, stopping in to make sure we're in our bunk beds. It is hard to go to sleep the night before we leave and go home. Suitcases are packed. Shoes and socks are set out in front of our lockers. Our traveling clothes have already been identified and matched according to the standards of the mid-1970s. The final farts sound off.

The great morning comes, the one I've prayed for, the day I go home. At the dining hall, the big breakfast isn't table style with table waiters but instead it is a buffet where you go through the line with a tray and get what you want put on your plate by the cooks behind counters. I get bacon, biscuits and gravy, scrambled eggs, and two cartons of chocolate milk. On the bus ride from Boys Ranch to Amarillo, I look out the window at the snow and daydream about what might happen. Maybe my mother will decide to keep me and I can go to their new church with cousin Perry, or maybe one of the aunts and uncles will convince my mother to let me live with them. My plan will be to work on Nana and the aunts and uncles, make them feel sorry for me with stories about bullies and George of the Water Tower and rattlesnakes and tarantulas. I'll tell them about getting your butt busted, picking vegetables and moving irrigation pipes, being tortured, that sort of thing. There's no way they will send me back, so bye-bye Boys Ranch. I'll only be coming back when I come to get Zappa and my stuff.

The bus pulls up at the Boys Ranch town office in Amarillo across from Ellwood Park. I take my suitcase and follow the other kids into the building. Big black-and-white photographs of Cal Farley and kids from a long time ago line the walls. We go downstairs to a big room with lots of couches and comic books and magazines where we wait to be taken to the bus station or to the airport. I flip through the newspaper that I find on the couch where I plop down. The title of a front-page story is "$167 a Month Doesn't Go Far." That's ridiculous. If I had that much money every month, I'd be rich.

I look up and see the man who picked me up at the bus station back when I got sent to Boys Ranch, the man who drove me out there.

"Hiya, squirt," he says.

"Hi."

He motions to the lady standing beside him. "Ken Arthur, let me introduce you to my wife, Gene."

The lady says, "Nice to meet you, Ken."

I stand up and shake her hand. "Nice to meet you."

Mr. Harriman tells me, "She's Cal Farley's daughter."

"Oh wow," I say. It makes her chuckle.

"Well, Merry Christmas," she tells me.

"Enjoy your family," says Mr. Harriman. "Be a good Boys Rancher and make us proud."

"I will."

They go around the room and talk to each boy and as they do, I watch boys' faces light up.

Later, when they take us to the bus station and I'm boarding my bus, Jeff Hostetter goes up the steps of the bus in front of me. He and I have been goofing off a lot together at the ranch. He looks at me and says, "Come on, we're sitting in the back." We go to the last seat, across from the bathroom. In a couple of hours, we pull into Childress, Texas, at a tiny bus station, and are allowed to get out for about twenty minutes until the bus takes off again. I buy an RC Cola out of the machine. Hostetter buys cigarettes from a man sitting on the sidewalk around the corner.

When the bus gets going, Hostetter strikes a match and lights a cigarette. "What?" he asks, blowing smoke up to the ceiling. "We're in smoking seats." He flips up the steel cover on the ashtray on his arm rest and hands me a cigarette. I take it and hold it between my first two fingers the way I saw Phyllis Diller hold her cigarette on the *Bob Hope Christmas Special*. He sucks on his cigarette so that the end glows and then he blows out the smoke.

"Get ready," he says.

He takes a match and lights the cigarette I've got sticking out of my mouth. I gag and cough and make distressed noises. The whole bus hears me. A couple of rows up, an old lady with a mean look stares back at us.

"You have to practice," Hostetter says. "Come on, try again."

I catch my breath and try another puff. More gagging and coughing, worse than before. A different old lady, with an even meaner look on her face, walks down the aisle toward us. She's about to go into the bathroom but turns to us and asks, "Do you mind?"

Hostetter and I look at each other and flick ashes into our ashtrays. She closes the door.

"Yes, we mind," Hostetter says, looking offended.

I adopt the offended look as well, adding, "Why yes, we do, thank you very much."

We start singing the song from the show *Scrooge*, "Thank you very much! Thank you very much! That's the nicest thing that anyone's ever done for me." When the lady comes out of the bathroom, we withstand her withering stare until she shakes her head and goes back to her seat, and then we go right back to smoking and ruining everyone's bus ride with hacking coughs.

When I get off the bus in Dallas, my Aunt Payo comes running toward me. She's got big hair piled up high and is wearing go-go boots and has a lot more daring eye makeup and personality than my mother does. After smothering me with kisses, she tells me that my mother and sisters are at home. They sent her to get me and bring me to the house. We get my suitcase and are soon in her car barreling out of downtown Dallas as I tell her all about the horrors of Boys Ranch. All she can say is, "You poor thing!" and, "Poor darling, that's terrible!"

I carry my suitcase and follow Aunt Payo up the sidewalk to the house my mother and sisters have moved to in Mesquite, a suburb of Dallas. She opens the door and announces, "We're here!" In the living room, there's a Christmas tree all lit up with lots of presents under it. My mother comes out from the kitchen and I drop the suitcase and run to her, crying and crying. I can't help it.

"Now, now," she says. "Girls, Bubba's here!" she calls out. Bubba is the only name my family has ever called me. My three sisters stand frozen in the hallway: Kim, the older one; Karyn, the one a couple of years younger than me; and Kellye, who's five.

"Well, come say hi to your brother."

They walk over to me and give me weak hugs and faint pats on my shoulder and say, "Hey, Bubba," in soft, quivering voices as if they are about to cry. I go to crying and the dam bursts and they cry with me and put their arms around me.

I get to sleep on the couch, which is the greatest thing in the world because I can look at the Christmas tree all night. It is the silver one I remember us having before I went to Boys Ranch, decked out with ornaments and lit by the color wheel that turns underneath it. Everything is so much better than being at the dorm. Here, I can go to the refrigerator anytime I want. If I want a pickle, I can just go get one. Same with olives and crackers and slices of bologna. Water out of the water fountain isn't the only option here in the free world like it is in the dorm. Our refrigerator has grape sodas and milk, chocolate milk even, and sweet tea. It feels like a religious experience when I look up into one of the kitchen cabinets and see Cap'n Crunch, Rice Krispies, Alpha Bits, and Sugar Crisp. Boys Ranch doesn't believe in cereal, another reason they should not send me back to that hell hole. Here, I can watch TV morning, noon, and night. I can go to the bathroom and shut the door and not be sitting on the throne next to other morons firing off turds.

My sisters have posted pieces of paper on their doors that say, "Do Not Enter. Knock First." When my mother goes to work, they keep their doors closed. I sit in the living room wondering what they're doing in their rooms. When they emerge, they're prissy and bossy.

"You need to turn the light off in the bathroom when you leave. Electricity is expensive."

"Leaving the toilet seat up is totally rude, you know."

"If I see you drink milk out of the jug again, I'm telling Mom."

"You can put your shoes outside if they stink so bad, you know."

"I'm telling Mom you said Raggedy Ann is dumb."

"Don't just take two ice cubes out of the tray. Dump it out in the bucket and fill the tray again. Don't you know anything?"

"If I hear you use Jesus's name in vain again, I'm telling Mom."

"You lost my black crayon. I'm telling Mom."

They threaten to tell on me at least a million times a day. My mother says if we don't straighten up, she's going to take all the presents under the tree back to the store. She's gone into debt and will never be able to pay it off, so we have to watch it, or she will take everything back. I try get on my sisters' good sides by playing Barbie dolls with them. This consists of taking the Barbie doll they give me, the one missing several fingers and toes and some hair, and going to a section of the living room beside the couch or along some section of the wall where I construct an apartment for the doll.

They tell me her name is Linda. I take some books, like encyclopedias, and prop them up to build walls. I take another fatter, smaller book for a bed and drape a washcloth over it and pretend that it's a bedspread. The sisters claim the best sections of the living room to make houses for their dolls and bring in toy furniture from their rooms. I want to borrow some of their toy furniture, but they say no, Linda is poor. We never actually play with the Barbie dolls. No, instead we spend an hour creating rooms for them and then explain to one another at the end what each room is and what the items in them are intended to be. That Band-Aid box with the piece of paper taped around it? Oh, that's the dresser, Kim tells me. The wooden block? She says that's the TV. When I show them the house I constructed for my deformed and disabled doll, poor Linda, they put on exaggerated frowns and shake their heads, disappear into their rooms and shut their doors.

Karyn and Kellye still believe in Santa Claus and so Kim and I get to stay up late on Christmas eve and help my mother bring in the gifts from Santa she has hidden in the trunk of her car. I wake up on the couch early in the morning as Karyn and Kellye hop up and down in front of the tree and run back and forth trying to get my mother to get up so they can open up all the presents. Kim gets a lot of girly stuff but also gets a Magic 8-Ball. I wish I had that. Karyn gets dolls and clothes and a spirograph. I ask if I can play with it later. She says maybe. Kellye gets Play-Doh and baby dolls and plastic ponies. When I rip the wrapping paper off my last gift and see what it is, I'm over the moon: a Six Million Dollar Man action figure. He's wearing a red tracksuit and has an engine block that you put in his right hand, pump the button on his back, and watch his bionic arm lift the engine over his head. I intone the sacred words, "Steve Austin, astronaut, a man barely alive. Gentlemen, we can rebuild him. We have the technology. We have the capability to make the world's first bionic man. Steve Austin will be that man. Better than he was before. Better, stronger, faster."

Aunt Payo and cousin Perry are coming over for Christmas dinner, so my mother and Kim declare the kitchen off limits as they prepare the dishes. I mainly stay in the backyard with the Six Million Dollar Man where the girls won't bug me, but they come out there regularly and are as annoying as all get-out. Karyn brings Kim's Magic 8-Ball outside and has me ask it a question. My question is, "Will I get my wish?"

Karyn shakes the magic eight ball and looks at the answer and reads it aloud, "Very doubtful."

Figures.

"What was your wish?" she wants to know. I'm not telling. She says she doesn't care anyway and goes back to the house. She also says I'm not allowed to play with her spirograph either.

"Fine!" I shout at her. I wouldn't let her touch the Six Million Dollar Man with a thirty-nine-and-a-half-foot pole, so she can just forget it.

Aunt Payo calls us to the table for the appetizer she's made: meatballs in a grape jelly and chili sauce. We use toothpicks as utensils to eat them. My mother also puts out her ambrosia, made from fruit salad, sour cream, whipped cream, and marshmallows. Supper's good, the glazed ham especially, but the other dishes not so much, especially that thing that had olives and sour cream and deviled ham with raisins. I run into the bathroom and spit it into the toilet.

We'll be going to Longview for the next couple of days, out to 202 where Nana and the whole family will be getting together.

202 is a house that my Aunt Dottie and the other relatives had transported from Longview to the deep woods outside of the city limits near Hallsville for family gatherings and holidays. It has the original house number 202 still on it, but it's down an asphalt road with no name as far as I know, and so we all just refer to it as 202. When I was little and my father still lived with us, we had a trailer in front of 202, out by the road. We had chickens there, and a dog named Happy, but my father kicked him one day and broke his leg and then we never saw the dog again.

There are already a lot of cars at 202 when we get there. Inside, it's packed with aunts and uncles and cousins claiming bunk beds and banging around in the kitchen. I run to Nana and she gives me a big hug and wants to know everything I've been doing. All the relatives gather around me and I'm so happy I can't stop crying when I see their faces again. They've made a shrine for Uncle Bill in the living room under the painting of Jesus praying in the garden. Uncle Bill died of cancer this past summer. They hold his picture up and make everybody notice how much I look like him. Uncle Lisle puts me on his lap and says I look more like him and we pose for a photograph.

A car honks out front and people exclaim, "Dottie's here!" We go out and watch Aunt Dottie pull up in a convertible with the top down, wearing fake vampire teeth. Her husband, Moe, wears a curly wig. Everybody swarms the car like they're seeing movie stars. My Aunt Bettye really does look like a movie star, though, with her elegant coiffed hair and poised demeanor. Her daughter, my cousin Debbie, is a knockout. They live across the street in a really nice brick house and a big barn with horses. There are several relatives that live close by: Aunt Hedy and Uncle Mercer live only about two miles away on a big ranch, and Uncle Lisle and Aunt Jean live up the road from 202 next to Uncle Ernest, who used to be married to Aunt Frances.

With everything going on, it's easy to be distracted from my main mission of getting the relatives alone one-on-one and giving them my sob story about the horrors of Boys Ranch. One of them will take me in, I just know it, but I'm not finding the chance to weave my web as the days go along. I get too mesmerized by the fire pit and the embers, by the hay rides and the red eyes of the Texas wolves we see looking at us through the pines, by the funny stories and jokes everybody is always telling, the huge suppers with everybody talking at the same time, the times we go exploring in teams led by one of our aunts, off to look for antiques in abandoned houses that we find in the deep woods. Every once in a while I get one of them alone and go into the butt bustings at Boys Ranch, the brutality of the child labor I've been forced to endure, the terror of being stalked by a one-armed man with a hook who fell off of the water tower, that kind of stuff, but I'm not making any breakthroughs. My only hope is with Nana. If I can get some time with her, I bet I can convince her to make my mother keep me or arrange it to where I can live with somebody in the family.

Time grows short. Some people will be going home soon. My mother will be taking me to the bus station in Longview, the same one she took me to when she sent me to Boys Ranch. Nana gathers all the children around her in the living room by Uncle Bill's shrine. We sing with her, "Jesus loves the little children, all the children of the world. Red and yellow, black and white, they are precious in his sight. Jesus loves the little children of the world." She reads to us from the Bible and leads us in prayer for Uncle Bill and all our family and for all the sinners in the world. When it's time for bed, the other kids scurry off, but I stay snuggled up beside Nana. I wait until the room clears out a little before I talk to her. Before I start, though, she says to me, "I'm so proud of you."

"You are?"

"Yes."

"Why?"

"Because you're so brave. You're doing so good at that Boys Ranch."

"I am?"

"Yes, indeed, and I love the letters you write to me, telling me how you're making straight A's, and riding in the rodeo. It's amazing what you're doing!"

"Oh yeah?"

"Fishing and camping and hiking and riding horses! It makes me so happy to hear about all the adventures you're having." She pulls me tight and kisses my forehead. "And that sweet, sweet poem, 'One Little Lamb.'"

Well, crap. I'm striking out.

The next day I'm on the bus headed back to Boys Ranch.

Chapter Seven

When the Prices' time is up for being our dorm parents, they move to a house by the dairy barn, where Mr. Price takes charge of all the horticulture at the ranch and Mrs. Price keeps working with Nurse Vandergriff at the infirmary. First we got a couple of substitute dorm parents that wash out after a month or two, but now we've got Mr. and Mrs. Little and things are calming down. Razzberry and I use our charms on Mrs. Little and work our way into her kitchen as helpers and tasters.

After five years at the ranch, Razzberry and I have pretty much gotten the hang of it. No more table waiting. Razzberry's got a job running tractors and working the livestock on the other side of the ranch. I'm the manager of the gym, all of it: the pool, the basketball court, the dodgeball and handball courts, the weight room, all the locker rooms, the secret upstairs supply room where candy for the concession stand is stored. Yes, I have keys to all of the doors. I can let myself into the gym, lock the door behind me, and go shoot basketball and nobody would know. I can go in the office and make phony phone calls to people in the phone book. It could be a great job, but usually I'm too busy sweeping and mopping and cleaning up and washing towels and jock straps. Too busy cleaning toilets and showers and floors. And more laundry. More drying. More folding. More sweeping followed by more mopping. They say I'm the manager. Yeah, I'm managing to do all the work. On top of that, there's a whole other job I have to do. One of my sub-duties involves being the manager of the Boys Ranch varsity football team. I get to go to all the games and run out on the field and get the tee after the kickoff, and be the water boy, and load up all the gear, and wash and dry their laundry. I'll tell you what I am managing: all the crap that has to be done.

I've been wanting to win a spot as a junior rodeo clown for a long time. Every rodeo season I try out and accumulate points throughout the summer practice sessions, but I've never made it yet, never scored high enough. Two weeks before Labor Day, on the big bulletin board in the dining hall, they post the names of the boys who made the cut in all the rodeo categories—broncs, bulls, steers, calves, trick riding, and junior and senior clowns.

The names posted are the ones that get to be in the official Boys Ranch Rodeo where the stands are full of people, where riding clubs from all over the Texas Panhandle and from Oklahoma and New Mexico come to the ranch and camp out at the rodeo grounds and ride in the Grand Entry Parade and fill the arena. Trophies and ribbons are handed out. The kids who get to be clowns have the most fun of all. They get makeup on their faces and wear wigs and clown costumes. They perform in the arena with everybody watching as they stand close by the gate-puller and when the gates are flung open and the cows come out bucking, they stay ahead of the cows so they get chased and kids that get bucked off don't get trampled as much. The clowns do funny antics and chase each other riding stick horses. Visitors want to have their pictures taken with them.

Sometimes their picture gets put in the newspaper. Razzberry made it last year and was a junior clown. He was the belle of the ball. Clowning it up in the stands with the audience. Everybody talking about how cute he was. That was such a drag for me. So this year I'm praying to Jesus and the whole Trinity that I see my name on the bulletin board.

The Trinity comes through. My name is on the list for junior clowns and steer-riding. I scream, "Yes!" and dance like I'm being electrocuted. Back at the dorm I cue a forty-five record on my record player and turn up the volume and sing Barry Manilow's "I Write the Songs." Razzberry comes in my room and howls like a coyote as I sing. I belt it out: "I write the songs that make the whole world sing." Cue the howling. "I write the songs of love and special things." Razzberry again howls right at his mark. People threaten to kill me if I don't shut up and turn it off. Jealous losers trying to take away my glory.

I sit at the table in my room and write a letter to my girlfriend to tell her about being selected for junior clowns. I prop up her picture in front of me to make people jealous when they walk past. I met her at BMA camp in the summer down in Ringgold, Louisiana. Bible Memory Association. If you sign up to be in BMA they give you a book of Bible verses based on what grade in school you're in and you memorize those verses and go down to the Sunday school every week and recite that week's verses to one of the monitors. If you get through all eight weeks, you get prizes and get to go to BMA camp in the summer. For the last four years I've memorized all eight weeks' worth of verses and have gone down and recited them all in one session. Nobody's ever done that. Then for all the weeks that follow, when everybody else is at the chapel waiting to recite their verses, I'm back at the dorm fishing or down at the gym eating candy bars in secret in the storage room. People think I'm a genius the way I recite everything at one time. It's best to let them think that.

Bible Memory Camp is fun because there are so many girls there. It's a whole week away from the ranch, sleeping in little cabins on a lake, riding pedal boats, canoeing, playing miniature golf and horseshoes, and a whole lot of church-going and praying and singing songs. I met the most beautiful girl there and she gave me her picture and her address so I could write her letters. Paige DiMaggio. I have the letters she's sent me in a pile so people will know it's serious. She's from San Augustine, Texas. I tell people she's related to Joe DiMaggio even though I have no idea if she is or isn't. Half of the idiots here don't even know who Joe DiMaggio is. Have you ever seen the Mr. Coffee commercial? I ask them. That's him. Have you ever heard the Simon and Garfunkel song "Mrs. Robinson"? The part where it goes, "Where have you gone, Joe DiMaggio, our nation turns its lonely eyes to you? Ooh, ooh, ooh." No? Figures. That's him they're singing about. Forget it. There's no use casting your pearls before these swine. Once I marry Paige DiMaggio, we'll drink coffee every day and they can go on being losers, nobody cares.

Labor Day weekend comes and I go down to the drama hall. The other two junior clowns and I try on different costumes and wigs and get our faces painted up. Everywhere we go, we're treated like celebrities. We get to cut in the bar-b-que line. We roam through the stands among the people filing in before the rodeo starts and ham it up with the folks. I run across this old man named Mr. Seymour who I remember from last rodeo. He's a big Boys Ranch donor, some rich guy from Utah. Last year I sold Cokes in the stands and he gave me a big tip, like two dollars, and also gave me and Zappa a ride in his car back to the dorm when the rodeo was over. He wrote me letters and sent me a colorful hat from Peru with knitted earflaps and tassels. There's no way I would ever wear it. He sent me a bag of dog food for Zappa. He's happy to see that I'm a clown this year. What a nice man. Maybe he'll adopt me and I'll live happily ever after in the country like Oliver Twist.

People buy me Cokes and Sno-cones and have their picture taken with me. I go over to the VIP boxes and make time with Mrs. Gene Farley Harriman—daughter of Cal and Mimi Farley, who started Boys Ranch—and Mr. Harriman, the man who picked me up from the bus station when I first got sent here. They want to hear about everything I'm doing. They have a way of making me feel special when I'm with them because they're interested in me. I bet they're interested in all the boys though, and that's what makes them the greatest people in the world.

I love it when rodeo starts. Dozens of riding clubs and their flags march into the arena. We all take off our hats and cover our hearts as Mrs. Price stands at a microphone in the upstairs booth and sings the national anthem. Then the riders carrying the Texas flag and the United States flag kick their spurs and ride their horses fast around the arena, crossing one another in the middle. It's the best rodeo ever. The cowboys on their horses. The riders in their chutes, cinched up, ready to go. All the action. The crowd roaring. All the beautiful people.

I exert every bit of energy I have running in the dirt, staying just ahead of the cows, anticipating which way they're going to move, protecting the riders, a clown's clown from the second the gate is pulled open, because I do make some special moves and dances that excite the audience. How many lives do I save? There's really no way of knowing. How many faces do I rescue from being permanently dented in the shape of hooves? Imagine going through life with the middle of your face smashed in, exactly in the shape of a hoof. Not good. And then imagine all the brain damage I just prevented from the trampling and carnage that would've happened had I not used my skills to bend those cows to my will, the fruitful lives that can now be lived, the grandchildren that will be born, the diseases that will be cured. There's really no way of knowing the magnitude of what I did today, but I'm sure it's major.

When the rodeo's over, everybody heads back to their dorms. I carry my wig because it's too hot to wear. Razzberry explains to me why he didn't do very good at junior bull-riding. I tell him excuses I have for steer-riding, why I fell off the second the gate opened. Mr. Seymour sees me and pulls his car over. Razzberry and I get in the back, but Mr. Seymour tells me to come sit in the front, so I do.

"You did such an excellent job!" Mr. Seymour says, leaning over to hug me and pat my shoulder. "Superb."

I introduce him to Razzberry in the back, but he's very excited to see me and keeps patting me on the shoulder and the leg. "Master Kenneth, where's your dog?"

"He's running around smelling everything probably."

"Did you get the dog food I sent?"

"Oh, yes sir, thank you."

He hugs me and pats me on the head and shoulders and leg. "And the hat from the Peruvian highlands?"

"Yes sir, thank you."

"Did you like it?"

"Oh yes. It's great."

"Good." More hugging and patting.

He eventually drives the car and takes us up to Anderson Dorm. We get out but he calls me back wanting to tell me something and I get in again. He motions for me to move closer as if he has a secret he wants to tell me.

"I'm going to send you some books. You like good books?"

"Yes sir, I sure do." Good comic books, that's about it, but I can't tell him that.

He puts his arm around me and pulls me closer and whispers, "These are special books, antiques. Written at the end of the last century."

"What kind of books are they?"

"Adventure stories by George Alfred Henty. You must never loan them out or discard them. They're very old and the longer your keep them, the more valuable they become."

"Okay."

He says some more stuff and hugs me again and kisses me on the forehead for some reason even though I have on clown makeup. I escape his car and wave goodbye.

Razzberry stands there waiting. He asks, "Who is that? Why was he petting you like Zappa?"

"Who cares why? He's rich and guess what? If I asked him to adopt us, I bet he would in two seconds."

"You maybe, not me."

"He'd have to. We're brothers."

"That's the man that sent you that stupid hat?"

"It's not stupid. It's from Peru." I go past him and inside to take off my clown makeup.

I have second thoughts about asking Mr. Seymour to adopt us when I get the first book in the mail from him, *Beric the Briton: A Story of the Roman Invasion* by G.A. Henty, published in 1892. Alarm bells go off as I read the first lines in the preface. "My Dear Lads: I felt that a series of stories dealing with the wars of England would be incomplete did it not include the period when the Romans were masters of the country." I think, oh no.

So I skip the preface. I never read prefaces anyway. I go to chapter one and read, "It may be a fair sight in a Roman's eyes, but nought could be fouler to those of a Briton. To me, every one of those blocks of brick and stone weighs down and helps to hold in bondage this land of ours; while that temple that they dared to rear to their gods, in celebration of their having conquered Britain, is an insult and a lie."

I turn to a random page to see if it gets any better. "Boduoc would be waiting for him and he could not hurry over his visit, the first he had paid since his absence; therefore he pushed on, with scarce a glance at the stately temple of Claudius, the magnificent baths or other public buildings, until he arrived at the villa of Caius Muro, which stood somewhat beyond the more crowded part of the town."

Three strikes, you're out. I tuck the book away. Mr. Seymour sends more books as time goes on, all by G.A. Henty, and I quietly put them in my locker behind my blue jeans and never look at them.

During marching season, I'm busy being manager of the varsity football team and also in the marching band. Every half time I have to run and get my saxophone and put on my band uniform—white felt cowboy hat, fancy vest with the Boys Ranch branding logo on it and tassels coming off the shoulders, white spats over the shoes—and make it to the end zone, where the band is ready to march onto the field and wow the crowd with "Rhinestone Cowboy" and the theme song to *Hawaii Five-O*. After marching season, Mr. Pimpsell has me switch over from the alto sax to the oboe, which is hard to play because of the double reed but the notes are similar to the sax so I figure it out.

I'm not getting any better at piano for some reason, but my piano teacher, Mrs. German, one day brings a sheet of music that she wants to play and words in Latin that she wants me to sing. She's heard me sing before because she plays piano for the choir I'm in. Mr. German, the choir director, says I have a good singing voice and that I'm the best soprano in the choir. But I sing the song, and she coaches me on how to pronounce the Latin words and how to roll my r's, like when I sing the word requiem. Rolling your r's is like a slight drum roll with your tongue, she says, and has to be a bit understated and not too pronounced. I act like I understand what she's saying and sing the way she wants me to. We spend the whole piano lesson with her teaching me how to sing this song in Latin. "Pie Jesu, Domine. Dona eis requiem. Sempiternam requiem. Dona eis requiem."

When I come back the next week she again sits at the piano and plays the same song and has me sing it over and over. She stops me every now and again and corrects how I say the Latin words, tells me to sing from my abdomen, not my throat. I act like I know what she's saying and keep trying to sing the song the way she wants me to. The song has one really high note and she's pleased with the way I hit that note, but I'm still singing from my throat and from not my abdomen.

She tells me that this is all about getting me ready to try out for a solo, that there's going to be a competition with boys from all over the area—Texas, Oklahoma, New Mexico, and Kansas—to see which boy will win the single spot to sing a solo with the Amarillo Symphony Orchestra and the Amarillo Symphony Choral Society at an Easter concert at the coliseum downtown. She says that she and Mr. German both think I have a good shot at winning the solo even though there will be a lot of competitors. This song, "Pie Jesu," is the one I have to sing in the tryouts and is the song that the boy soprano solo will sing in the coliseum with a full orchestra behind him on the day of the Easter concert.

"So let's start again from the top," she says, and I sit up straight as she perches her hands above the piano keys.

Chapter Eight

Mr. and Mrs. German take me one day in their car to Amarillo for the try out. We have an appointment at the symphony conductor's home. I meet the conductor, Thomas Conlin, who lived in New York City and was the director of the Queens Orchestral Society. He is originally from Washington, D.C. and later worked for the Chamber Opera Society of Baltimore and the National Ballet Society, the Goldovsky Opera Theatre, the North Carolina Symphony, and New York's Lincoln Theatre for the Performing Arts. The conductor's wife is elegant and refined, and everyone is graceful as they greet one another. We sit in their living room by their grand piano.

"Tell us about yourself," the conductor says. When I seem to draw a blank, he prods me. "Things you're interested in, activities you've been doing."

"Well, I got a pig a month ago."

"Oh." The conductor and his wife look at each other and seem eager to know more.

"It's a lot of work nobody told me about, honestly," I tell them. "Always having to change out the sawdust in his pen, for one thing. Pigs poop a lot and if you don't change out the sawdust, here come the maggots, so you're forever bringing wheelbarrows full of sawdust over."

"Fascinating," the conductor says.

"I'm hoping he'll be a show pig and I can take him to fairs and compete for ribbons. That will be awesome. After this, though, I'm getting a calf."

They look so pleased and happy, you'd think I just told them I went to Mars and back over the weekend. So I give them more. "I found an Indian grinding stone, a Kiowa Indian big flat rock they call a mortar and the stone in the middle, the pestle. It's what Indians used to grind, you know, stuff they needed to grind. They're putting it in the museum at Boys Ranch."

"You found this?" the conductor's wife asks.

"Yes. I go down the hill from the dorm a certain way all the time, planting my foot on the root of this yucca plant to pivot and go down to the spillway. Well, one day the yucca plant gave way and got uprooted because I kept landing on it. And so when my boot hit on the rock under it, I got down and uncovered it. Mr. Powell came and took a look and said it was from the Indians."

"That is amazing!" the conductor and his wife exclaim.

"Ken is in the Boys Ranch band," Mr. German wisely interjects. "He plays the alto saxophone and the oboe."

"And he's one of my piano students," says Mrs. German.

The conductor's eyes light up and he takes a new look at me. Mrs. German asks if I'm ready and goes to the piano. I get up and go stand by her. Singing the song to Mrs. German, just me and her in the piano room at Boys Ranch is one thing, but here, in this living room with the conductor and his wife and Mr. German sitting there looking at me, this is something else. I'd rather face Mrs. German but she already told me that I have to face them instead. It's late in the afternoon and the sun is coming in at a low angle, so I stand in a golden beam of sunlight so I can't see the people very well and maybe won't be as nervous.

Mrs. German sets the sheet music on the piano. Adjusts the seat. It's so quiet. Her hands are poised above the keys. She looks at me and gives me a quick wink and a smile. I nod that I'm ready, and she begins with the prelude.

I sing Gabriel Fauré's song "Pie Jesu" in Latin. It means "merciful Jesus" and asks God to grant eternal rest, the kind of haunting, sacred song you might hear at a funeral.

We stop for cheeseburgers on the way back to Boys Ranch, and Mr. German tells me that twenty-five boys are trying out for the solo, boys from glee clubs and choirs from the whole Tri-State area. Mrs. German says she is proud of me. She tells me that the conductor said I did an excellent job and that they wouldn't be surprised if I'm the one that gets chosen. We won't know for two weeks.

In the meantime, I have to work and slave for this pig of mine. I don't know who's out there telling people that pigs are smart, but I beg to differ. You can't teach my pig anything. Zappa can do a million tricks and he comes when you call him. Not this pig. What's more, he has no personality and he's outgrown the cute phase. Razzberry says that if Charlotte's web was above my pig pen it would spell out dumb pig instead of some pig. He thinks he's funny. He says he thinks I got a show pig, as in, "Show it to the butcher." Hardy-har-har. He says my pig is no fun to be around, that he's a boar.

He's coming up with jokes left and right as he and I throw rocks at birds that have come into the pig barn and are up in the rafters.

When we run out of rocks, we go out and get a new handful. We're supposed to be shoveling sawdust and cleaning out poop, but this is too much fun. Then, as I'm getting more rocks, out of the corner of my eye I see movement. It's Mr. Merle—the man in charge of the barns, who's got to weigh three hundred pounds—running across a field straight for us. Razzberry comes out.

"Cheese it," I tell him and drop my rocks. "It's Merle. He heard."

We take off running the back way, behind a grain bin and the lean-tos for the big sows. We make for the tree line at Big Morris Lake, angling over so we stay out of Mr. Merle's line of sight, and then from there it's a short run to the safety of the dorm.

We go about our business in the dorm, but we're like dead men walking with that sense of foreboding and impending doom. I go to the window and look out, expecting to see Mr. Merle's truck pull up. We keep hoping maybe he couldn't see who we were and can't positively identify us. The anxiety builds. Here I am on the cusp of a major singing career, when it's all going to be wiped out because of some birds in a pig barn? Since when is it a crime to throw rocks at birds? This isn't fair. Please, God, Merciful Jesus. Pie Jesu Domine.

Mr. and Mrs. Little call out for us to muster in the Big Room, everybody in the dorm. Oh no. This is it. We all file in and sit on the couches and chairs. Mr. and Mrs. Little stand at the front by the fireplace. Razzberry and I sit together by the trophy case. I bet Mr. Little is going to say he got a call from Mr. Merle and that we were seen throwing rocks in the pig barn. Our initial plan will be to deny it.

Instead, Mr. Little says he got a phone call from Mr. German, who said that he got official word from Amarillo that I was the one selected to sing the solo. It's like victory from the jaws of defeat. The Littles start clapping and get the guys to applaud, but a lot of them flap their hands together like tranquilized seals and make faces at me.

"Why don't you take a bow?" says one of the sour faces.

"Why don't you shut up?" I say.

One day, Razzberry finds out about the song I'm to sing, "Pie Jesu." He says he saw a movie where priests walked around a village chanting "Pie Jesu Domine" and hitting themselves in the head with books. He demonstrates by taking a book and putting a towel over his head like a hooded robe and walking around chanting in monotone, "Pie Jesu Domine." He hits himself in the forehead with the book and chants it again, "Pie Jesu Domine," and bangs the book into his forehead.

"You're lying. What movie was this?"

"*Monty Python.*"

"Never heard of it."

"It's about knights going to look for the Holy Grail and they gallop around pretending to be on horses and they use coconuts to make sounds for the horses' hooves."

"You're making it up. There's no way."

"Okay then, bet me."

"I'm not betting you. Get away from me."

Razzberry's not the kind to just let it go. Every week when I go down to practice the song with Mrs. German, he drops his voice and chants, "Pie Jesu Domine" and hits himself in the head either with his hand or whatever is nearby. Sometimes he just does it out of the blue. He's got other guys in the dorm doing it. Such an asshole.

Saturday, April 23, 1977. The day of the Easter Concert. I'm at the coliseum and have on the tuxedo they got tailored to fit me. I just combed my hair for twenty minutes to get it perfect, but it's still not. I wait in the wings backstage with the man who's to sing the baritone solo looking spiffy in his tuxedo. You can hear the audience rustling and talking as the instruments in the orchestra get tuned, violins and violas and bassoons, the cellos and English horns. I peek through the curtain at the audience. Looks like a lot of people. It is weird knowing the whole dorm is out there in the seats along with paying customers. Razzberry's out there. He told me when I start singing I should listen for him hitting himself in the head. I told him to use a knife.

A hundred people in the Amarillo Choral Society choir file past me in their robes and go onstage and take their places behind the orchestra. Mrs. Price goes by and smiles at me. She's in the choir and is the best singer I've ever heard. I'm a little nervous. The baritone soloist checks to make sure I'm ready and then I follow him onstage. We go in front of the orchestra as the audience applauds and then we take our seats below the conductor's stand. The applause ratchets up again when Mr. Conlin, the conductor, enters the stage and goes to his podium and turns and bows to the audience. I am just blown away. I have to hold myself in check when a tear leaks out because of the beauty and the joy and the feeling of the moment.

Seeing the conductor sway and move and direct the orchestra and the choir is mesmerizing from this nearby vantage point. His hands go this way and that way and swirl back and punctuate the air and reach out to the orchestra and control the players and their volume and intensity with his movements and his will. He is one with the music, and I am awed in a way I have never been in my life. When it's my time, I stand and go to the microphone and sing

THE SALT & PEPPER GANG

my song. Then there's the applause. It's surreal.

After Gabriel Fauré's "Requiem," with my "Pie Jesu" solo, the conductor leads the orchestra and the choir in Joseph Haydn's frenetic up-tempo "Te Deum" with Latin words flying out of the choir members' mouths, sounding like music that you'd only ever hear in heaven sung by angels.

After the concert, the conductor congratulates me and tells me to go up to the front of the coliseum by the doors and shake people's hands as they leave. Along the way, I meet up with Razzberry and he goes with me. We stand at the front as the people go by and sure enough, several old ladies want to stop and shake my hand and have me sign their programs. One of them hands me a pen from her purse. She says she's sure that one day I will be a famous singer. I sign my name on the program and Razzberry has his hand out, like maybe he wants to see it, so I hand him the lady's program. He takes the pen from me before I know what's happening and signs his name beside mine and smiles and hands the program back to the lady. She's super excited.

Razzberry and I laugh and cut up over us signing autographs at the coliseum. Men come over and shake our hands. Other ladies want their programs signed and soon we have a line going. One lady asks Razzberry who he is. He says he's the manager.

Finally they're mostly gone and people are ignoring us. Razzberry takes one of the programs sitting on a table and looks in it. He says, "Get this," and reads aloud in a phony voice what's written.

Soloist Ken Arthur, soprano, is 13 years old and an 8th grade resident of Cal Farley's Boys Ranch. He is a member of the Crusader Choir and a piano student of Mrs. Alice

German. In addition to his interest in music, Ken is a promising writer – having already completed three full length books! His former home is in Dallas.

"I didn't know they were going to put that in there," I say to him.

"What was that first book?"

"That was the one about the kid who found a crashed UFO with a robot in it and then took control of it and had all these adventures."

"What about the second one?"

"*The Red Vapor.*"

"What was that one about?"

"This red vapor comes from outer space to the Earth and shrinks everybody down to like two or three inches tall."

"It just shrinks the people?"

"Yeah."

"What about their clothes?"

"Yeah, their clothes too."

"Just what they're wearing or all the clothes, like stuff in the laundry and sitting in stores?"

"I don't remember. Who cares, anyway? The story is not about the clothes, it's about their adventures. The point is, they're suddenly tiny people and everything else is still big, like phones and cars and dogs."

"Why should their clothes shrink if nothing else does?"

"Will you shut up about their clothes?"

"I think you should make the clothes stay the same size and everybody's suddenly three inches tall and also naked."

"No! God, you're dumb."

"What about the third book?"

"*The Army of Snakes*."

"I'm going to guess that it's about an army of . . ."

"The government, see, has this facility in the desert with all these snakes from all over the world. Thousands and thousands of snakes. Like hundreds of thousands."

"What are they doing with all the snakes?"

"I don't know, ask the government. So anyway, the snakes get out. There's a failure of the system and they all go toward this town."

"The army of snakes?"

"Shut up."

"What do the snakes do?"

"What the hell do you think snakes do, they bite and they kill."

"I think that you should have the three-inch-tall naked people fight the snakes."

"We're no longer friends, me and you."

A husband and wife come over to us, so we straighten up and try to act like movie stars.

Chapter Nine

It's a gray day in October but it's Razzberry's fifteenth birthday and there's going to be a party with cake and ice cream at Anderson Dorm tonight, so that's something to look forward to at least. Razzberry gets to invite a couple of guys from other dorms and I've heard he's invited my buddy Ty Lightfoot from Jeffries Dorm and Chris Rattan, who is one of the staff kids, but I don't know who else. This morning, people at the dining hall were talking about the Yankees beating the Dodgers in the World Series last night. I don't care about baseball. It's so boring. I only care about the Dallas Cowboys. We're undefeated heading into this week. Razzberry's Steelers have already lost two games. Roger Staubach is so much better than Terry Bradshaw, there's no question. Plus Razzberry's from Port Arthur, so shouldn't he be a Houston Oilers fan? Why is he glomming on to the Steelers except for getting on their bandwagon?

This is what I think about sitting in FFA class instead of paying attention. Future Farmers of America. We're going over the FFA motto. The creed. The code of ethics. There's no class that could interest me less. I try to draw a football helmet on a piece of paper. It looks misshapen. I'm not satisfied with it and start erasing.

Mr. Dugger, the school principal, pokes his head in the door and says he needs to see me. Everybody looks at me thinking I'm in trouble. I have no idea what this could be about. I'm a straight-A student. Nobody I ever knew got called to the office by the principal himself, so what could I have done? I get up and go out the door and follow him down the hall, listening to the clicking and clacking of our footsteps as we go past the lockers and classrooms to his office. I sense doom.

Mr. Little is waiting there. He tells me that my mom is taking me out of Boys Ranch. She's up at the Boys Center right now waiting to take me away. They've already packed up all my things from my locker at the dorm and Mr. Little has everything in a box in his truck. Mr. Dugger hands me my transcript and tells me to give it to my mother so I can be enrolled in school wherever I'm going.

I go in the truck with Mr. Little down to the Boys Center by the entrance to Boys Ranch. My mom's car is parked out front. We go inside, and they take me to Mr. Waldrip's office. He's the biggest administrator there is, I think. He gives me a check for the money I had in the Boys Ranch bank. Twenty-six dollars. I also get a check of the proceeds from my pig, a hundred and fifteen dollars. I am rich. Too bad that pig is going to the butcher. If only he had listened to me.

Outside, my mom is on the lawn talking to Mr. Little and other Boys Ranch men in a huddle. She keeps shaking her head no at them. I wonder what they're asking her, what she's saying no about. Mr. Waldrip waits with me on the porch, his hand on my shoulder while the others talk out in the yard.

Mr. Price's truck comes down the road and pulls up beside my mom's car. He gets out wearing his big cowboy hat and goes around and opens the tailgate. Out jumps Zappa. From nowhere, tears come out because how could I be forgetting Zappa? How could I be so dumbstruck at what's going on that I forget my dog and go off somewhere without him? I go down the steps on the grass and Zappa comes running to me and jumps into my arms wagging and licking my tears. Mr. Price comes over and tells me to be good and make him proud. I tell him thank you for bringing Zappa and he tousles my hair. The real significance of what is happening starts to hit me when I look up at Mr. Price, the man who raised me for so many years and taught me how to cast a fishing pole, how to reel it in, how to tie a fishing knot, how to throw a baseball and bridle a horse and put on a saddle and ride rodeo and be a good person in life: Mr. Price, the greatest man I ever knew, saying goodbye to me.

Mr. Price and Mr. Waldrip go to Mr. Little and the other men who are talking to my mom on the grass. Zappa and I get my cardboard box out of Mr. Little's truck and put it in my mom's car. I open the back door and Zappa jumps in, me behind him. My mom, her mouth in a frown, gets in and puts it in reverse.

"Well, you finally get to come home," she says, "but we are not allowed to have a dog. I tried to tell them but they're making us take him. We're going to have to figure something out, but let's just go home."

Zappa and I sit in the back seat with my box and look out the rear window as we go through the Boys Ranch gate. I look back at the group of men on the lawn, at Mr. Price and Mr. Little raising their hands goodbye. We go down the lonely road past Boot Hill Cemetery to the Boys Ranch stone pylon and turn on the highway towards Amarillo, forty miles away.

My mom talks to me, but I don't hear half of what she's saying because I'm reeling and in disbelief that I'm actually leaving. She talks about my aunts and uncles and things they did that made her pack up and move from Dallas to Amarillo without telling anybody and that she's not having anything to do with them anymore, not with anybody in the family. She says my older sister ran away and went to live with either my father in Houston or one of my cousins or maybe she's getting married even though she's still in high school, something. It's hard to listen to the stream of words flying out of her mouth at me and Zappa, so many words come so fast, like out of a fire hose. Sometimes minutes go by as I look out the window and forget she's talking and have no idea what she's been saying. My mind is on Razzberry and not being able to say goodbye, on his birthday no less. And what about all my other friends like Tim Smith and David Rayburn and Ty Lightfoot and the guys in my class? I don't get to say goodbye to anybody?

I look in the box. It's just my clothes and those stupid books by G.A Henty that Mr. Seymour sent me and the hideous hat from the Peruvian highlands. Where's my shoebox of all my letters from Paige DiMaggio? Where's her picture? They're not here. What about my fishing pole and my tackle box? My bicycle? We could've put my bike in the trunk and strapped it down, that wouldn't be a problem. What about my skateboard? What about my chess game? What about my saxophone and my oboe? I mean, everything happened so fast. I'm wondering, are we ever going to go back and get everything? I want to break in on my mom's monologue and tell her that they didn't get all my stuff, but she's on a rant about how we are not to mention my older sister ever again and we are never to mention my father's name. I know his name. It's George. But now he's the devil, she says, and we can never say his name again.

No one in the family can know where we are, she tells us. We're on our own from now on. She used to trust this one relative and then this other one, and she says this person said or did something terrible and that's why she's through with the family. All the relatives are teaming against her. She's a fast talker with no need for breaths and so there's no way to break in on her to tell about my things and that we need to go back to Boys Ranch and get them. I have to wait and keep listening to what she's saying, thinking I'll get a chance eventually after she get this stuff out about the relatives and my sister who ran away and Elvis dying in August and her blood pressure and her bills and everything. Thank God I have Zappa. He's coming with me. So we sit in the back with the window halfway lowered and fly down the road to Amarillo.

We go to a two-bedroom house they've rented. I have to share a room with my younger sister. The youngest one sleeps in the other room with my mom. The older sister, Kim, ran away, so she's out. We're not allowed to say her name either. We can't say the names Kim or George. There's a huge fenced-in backyard for Zappa plus a garage for him in the colder days. I'm to be enrolled in Sam Houston Junior High School in the ninth grade and walk to and from school every day. It seems exciting to me in some ways because of being in the free world for one thing and being in a school with girls for another and being able to watch TV and go to a refrigerator for whatever I want, all this is new.

My two sisters and my mom are like strangers to me, though, and I'm like a stranger to them. It's awkward. I'm not sure any of them actually like me, not even my mom, because she's just kind

of cold and distant and preoccupied with her worries. I don't blame
her, because it takes a lot of money to move from Dallas to Amarillo
and to pay for me and my food and stuff and how depressed she
is over my sister running away and whatever she says her family
did to her, my aunts and uncles, even my grandmother. It's a big,
convoluted story told with endless repetition.

Plus, we're poor so we can't always run the heater and have to
wear socks on our hands to keep them warm and wear multiple
pairs of pants and shirts and sleep under heavy covers. We turn on
the electric stove in the morning, the top burners and the oven, and
we warm up next to it like it's a fireplace.

Our TV is a black-and-white one with the picture tube going out.
The picture sometimes blows up to where you can't see what's going
on. So you have to go up to it and smack it on the side with your
hand, like Fonzie slaps the juke box on *Happy Days*, and the picture
tube snaps back and you can continue watching for a while until
you have to do it again. In the first two days at home, I watch more
TV than I ever did in all the years I was at Boys Ranch. *Get Smart*
is my favorite show. I also like *Bewitched*, but my mom doesn't let
us watch it because it's about witches and the devil and my mom
is a major Christian, even more than me. I really don't see how
Uncle Arthur and Dr. Bombay and Aunt Clara are evil, but we're
not allowed to watch it anymore after one of my sisters told on me.

Right away I know the answer about whether we are going to get
my things left behind at Boys Ranch or not. It's no, we're not. My
mom tells me it is part of life, losing things. Sam Houston Junior
High has a band. I want to be in the band but my mom says it costs
money to buy a saxophone and we don't have the money for that. I
ask for a fishing pole but she says I don't need one right now because

it's the winter and there's no place to fish anyway in Amarillo. What about Bible Memory Association and Bible Memory Camp and Paige DiMaggio, her letters and her picture? She tells me that only rich people send their kids to those kinds of camps and so no, there's not going to be any Bible Memory Camps in my future. We can't even pay our bills, she says. This means I'll never see Paige DiMaggio again. Doesn't anything matter to anybody except me? I'm supposed to just accept losing Paige DiMaggio forever? Plus my mom says there's a good chance we'll be moving to Lubbock because she's applying to be in civil service and wants to get a job at the Air Force Base down there. That means I'm never going to see Razzberry again or any of my Boys Ranch brothers.

The worst comes on day three after leaving Boys Ranch. After school, my sisters and I are watching *The Gong Show* and my mom comes home from work and makes us turn it off. She says to us, "We can't have the dog."

I fall apart right when I hear what she's said. We can't have the dog.

I breathe hard and try not to cry but it's hopeless. The bottom drops out and I start falling.

No, please, no. I beg her and sink to the floor. Please. Please. Don't take Zappa away from me. He's all I have. He's everything I have. Please, no. Please, Momma, please. I'll do anything. You can use the money from my pig to pay the landlord so we can keep him.

My mom says she already had to use that money for the light bill and for groceries. "It's best for the dog if he goes back to Boys Ranch and can run free," she says. "Besides, the landlord says we can't have pets. Get up off the floor."

She tells me that we're taking the dog back to Boys Ranch tomorrow and letting him out. That's all there is to it. "It's better than the dog pound, isn't that right?"

I'm curled up in a ball on the floor. There's no way out.

I sit with Zappa in the cold in the backyard until everybody is asleep. Lines from a poem we had to read at Boys Ranch come to my mind where it says "things fall apart, the center cannot hold," and something about the ceremony of innocence being drowned. It was by William Butler Yeats, I remember that much.

All the stars are out. I look up and pray to Jesus that he'll help me in my time of need. I put my hands together. I tell him I'm sorry for all the things I've done and that if he can help me I will spend all the rest of my life serving him and devoting my life to him, just please help me find a way to keep Zappa.

When it's late and everyone's asleep, I let Zappa in the house even though my mom doesn't allow it. Who cares anymore? I give him bologna slices from the refrigerator. We sleep in the living room on the floor next to each other side by side.

In the morning I head out to Sam Houston Junior High with my head down as I walk the sidewalks, looking down at my Boys Ranch boots that kids in my new school made fun of yesterday, but I don't have anything else except my dress shoes that I wear to church and there's no way I'm wearing those, and my tennis shoes that smell so bad and look so nasty. Yesterday some kid said to me in the lunch room, "Where you headed, Tex?" and pointed at my boots, laughing and getting other kids laughing at me. I've got my Boys Ranch buzz cut, unlike their city hair, and they laughed at it yesterday too. One of them said, "You're the squarest square since Isosceles made a triangle," and got everybody laughing. Hardy-har-har.

When I get home from school, I sit in the backyard with Zappa and wait for my mom to arrive from work. My stomach feels like it needs to throw up when the car pulls into the driveway. On the forty-mile ride to Boys Ranch I sit in the back with Zappa and don't say a word. I don't feel like talking ever again. I have the feeling that if my mom wanted me to have the dog she could have done something. It's a huge fenced-in backyard. He'd never come in the house. He doesn't dig holes. I'm the one that goes on turd patrol. What kinds of problems could he possibly cause? I'm suspicious that it's just my mom who doesn't want the dog and that she didn't even ask the landlord about it. Wish I could find out.

We get to Boys Ranch and turn on one of the dirt roads around back by the calf barn so people won't see. She pulls the car over and I hold Zappa one last time and put my face on his. I get out and pick him up and set him on the road. He doesn't understand when I get back in without him and he cocks his head looking at me.

We pull away and he starts running after the car. My mom hits the gas and we leave him behind running as fast as he can in a cloud of dust.

The phone rings one afternoon. My sister says it's for me. I'm shocked. It's the first phone call I ever got. It's Mr. Seymour. He says he found out from the Boys Ranch Town Office that I was taken out of the ranch. He's visiting from Utah and heard I live in Amarillo and wanted to come by my house and see me.

Why, sure.

My mom's at work and she won't care. Mr. Seymour is rich. Maybe he'll marry her and we'll all be rich. Maybe he'll help me get Zappa back, help me pay money to the landlord. I might have to deal with some more G.A. Henty books, but hopefully he'll never quiz me about them and will never know that I find them completely unreadable.

I don't let my sisters know Mr. Seymour's coming over. They'll cause a scene. They're watching *Gilligan's Island* when I see his car pull up in the driveway and I stand ready at the door when he knocks. I give him a hug and tell my sisters that he's my friend. They're petrified as he comes in and looks them over.

He wants to talk to me alone, so we go to my room, the one I share with the middle sister, and he shuts the door. I've prepositioned the unwearable Peru hat beside the G.A. Henty books on my shelf so he'll see them. He sits on the bed and I get up beside him. I start telling him about things that have been going on. I tell him about my solo at the coliseum with the orchestra and about my sister running away and how my mom is divorced and then I tell him about Zappa and how much I need to get him back. He sees me brokenhearted and hugs me and pulls me close as I keep telling him about how bad I felt when my mom made us take Zappa back to the ranch.

He hugs me some more and sits closer to me. I don't like feeling his breath on my neck or the way he strokes my hair with his hand. Then he kisses me on my ear and my neck. I jump up from the bed and back away from him because all of a sudden it hits me that he's a molester.

I tell him, "You have to leave."

I open the door and stand there. He says when he's in Peru the children all come around and sit on his lap and he gives them candy that they can't get down there and how much he loves helping children and making special friends.

"Mr. Seymour, you have to leave, OK?"

He looks at his watch and says he wished he had more time but that he has to run. He goes into the living room and pets my sisters on their heads and starts blathering something about studying the classics as their eyes slowly gravitate from him back to the TV and Gilligan and the Skipper. When he comes to the door he stoops down to say something to me and reaches out to touch my face but I back away and flash an angry face at him because I'm on the verge of exploding.

"Goodbye, Master Kenneth," he says, going through the door. "I've got your address now, so I'll send you another book, one of G.A. Henty's finest, a first edition, so you'll want to hold onto it."

He looks like he's about to say something else, but I close the door on him and latch the chain.

We move to a trailer park on the south side of Amarillo and I go to Canyon High School for the first two months of the tenth grade but then we move to Lubbock when my mom gets a job at Reese Air Force Base. We're outside the Lubbock city limits at Town and Country Mobile Estates, aka Mobile Mistakes, a shabby trailer park where we have roaches. They're everywhere. I get a job mowing lawns using the trailer park manager's riding mower. For weeks I drive it all over even though it's painfully slow. Then somebody tells me it has gears. I've been going everywhere and mowing all the yards in first gear. What must people be thinking? I retreat into my room where I read *The Lord of the Rings* and teach myself to juggle and listen to the *CBS Radio Mystery Theater* at night on my radio.

Tony Kennedy, the first victim of the Blue Max Club, graduated from Boys Ranch and lives next door since his mom is from around here. He's even taller, lankier, and looking more and more like

Ichabod Crane these days. We hatch a plan to tell my mom that he's taking me to Abernathy to meet Tony's mother and we'll be gone all day. Instead, we get in his 1974 Honda Civic and take off driving two and a half hours north to Boys Ranch. I want to see Razzberry and get Zappa. Everybody at Town and Country Mobile Mistakes has dogs. They roam all over and so I'm getting him and bringing him home, I don't care what my mom says. We'll say that Tony's mom went and got him for me and surprised us when we went to visit her. We can't admit to driving all the way to Boys Ranch and back because my mom would never let me hang out with Tony Kennedy ever again.

We get to Boys Ranch and go up to Anderson Dorm to ask around to see where Razzberry is. They say he's on the other side of the ranch somewhere driving a tractor or messing with cattle. It feels weird being inside the dorm again and walking down the hall, seeing all kinds of unfamiliar faces who showed up after I left. I ask about Zappa and they tell me that he died and they buried him at the pet cemetery. I turn away and walk fast out the door so nobody sees me crying.

Tony drives us over to the far side of the ranch to look for Razzberry. We never find him. I sit in silence most of the long drive to Lubbock and eventually crawl in the back and go to sleep.

Two months later, my mom meets a man through a Christian singles service and marries him. We pack everything into a U-Haul and move to Orlando, Florida, where the man lives. He's a maintenance worker for Eastern Airlines. We move into a house with an orange tree in the backyard and two palm trees in the front. My room is half of a converted garage and I never leave it except to go to the bathroom and the refrigerator. I get incarcerated at Colonial

High School and land a job cleaning tables and floors at the Chicken and Biscuit restaurant at Sea World.

After three months, my mom decides she hates the man she just married. When he's at work on a midnight shift at the airport, she gets a U-Haul and we leave in the middle of the night. She's got a job at Langley Air Force Base in Hampton, Virginia.

I curl up and try to sleep in the backseat as we head north, every mile going further from Texas than I've ever been. Maybe taking me out of Boys Ranch was a mistake. I felt like I belonged there. I had friends there. I had a brother.

Nothing feels right. I don't feel like the same me anymore. My fires have all died out.

Chapter Ten

It's 2005. Twenty-seven years have passed since I left Boys Ranch and last saw Razzberry. Not an insignificant period of time. I was fourteen back in 1977. I am forty-one now. The end of the seventies and then the eighties and the nineties went by. I became a dad and an ex-husband. September 11 happened. All the kids I knew at Boys Ranch grew up and fathered babies or died in explosions or from leukemia or something or other, or perhaps made it through and were successful somewhere out in the world, or, more likely, were eking it out in whatever corner of the world they ended up living. Young people think they'll be forever young. I know I did. There was no way I could image being forty-one years old. All of a sudden, though, I was. Time didn't seem to fly by. It was just all gone one day when I looked at the skin on my hands and took a long, hard look in the mirror.

I tried finding Razzberry several times when I went back to Texas over the years. Always felt like I needed to, that he was one of the missing pieces of my jigsaw puzzle. I walked up and down streets in Amarillo where people told me they thought he lived, seeing if I could spot the type of truck they said he drove. Many times I called directory assistance and wrote down the phone numbers of the Raymond Hills and R. Hills in the area code and rang all of them to see if he was one. No luck. When I went and asked, people at the Boys Ranch Town Office told me he used to take his little boy out to the ranch to fish all the time, so he has to be somewhere in the panhandle. I just have never been able to find him.

It's sad to say, but I don't have anything to do with my mother anymore. It just was never meant to be, me and my mom. Long story. I'll take the hit. I've never been back in touch with my large Texas family either, all those aunts and uncles and cousins that my mother estranged me from. I could never betray my mother by contacting the family she despised—she had such hostility toward them—and so they vanished into history along with everything else I used to have. I thought I needed to be the good son for all those years when I stayed firmly on her side, for her sake, and never tried to contact my big Texas family even though little of what she said made sense to me, the grudges, the hatred.

I'm separated from my wife of fourteen years. Headed into divorce court. The loss of daily contact with my two kids is what's been tough, not being there as the dad like I'd always been on an everyday basis, not seeing them in the mornings on their way to school, not being there to check their homework, not there to decorate the house for holidays. Not being there is what hurts. I push away the sadness of thinking that those days are gone, the days of taking them fishing, cooking on the grill in the backyard, watching them in the pool, and reading stories to them at bedtime. I wish they could be little forever and I could always be there in the eternal now, me and them together on a never-ending Christmas morning.

Not least of all is the fact that Chelsea, my thirteen-year-old daughter, has autism. I have been there every day of her life fighting for her, trying to pull her out of that black hole. She needs me. Kacey, my little boy, he's seventeen now, a little hard to handle, but he needs me too. I need them. That I know. Plus, right at the pivotal moment when my wife and I got a legal separation, two of my greatest friends in the world died, one right after the other. Non-Hodgkin's lymphoma took Jay Pertuso. A drunk driver hit Jerry Anders head on when Jerry was going home from work. I cried for months. More and more it feels like I'm sinking. Feels like everything's stagnant, the great wasteland of middle age suddenly upon me.

Today, however, is the day I've been waiting for. I'm in the truck headed north on Interstate 75 to Atlanta, where I'm picking Razzberry up at the airport. Britt Hammond, one of the guys in Anderson Dorm in the seventies, who's President of the Boys Ranch Alumni Association, called and gave me a phone number where I could reach him. Britt said he heard Razzberry was in pretty bad shape, that he had some sort of stroke and was taken down hard. He woke up one day with his body paralyzed, the whole left side. Luckily he got taken to the hospital, where they operated on him. He's not paralyzed anymore, but he needs a cane to walk and has a lot of medical problems. They say it's some sort of degenerative spinal thing that's never going to go away.

When I got Razzberry on the phone the other day, he said that he was living with a friend of his named Rose and her husband and their fourteen dogs. I could barely hear what he was saying because of the barking. He told me to hold on and turned to the dogs and screamed bloody murder to shut them up. He said when Rose and her husband are at work, he's supposed to keep the female dogs separated from the male dogs by a kiddie fence between the kitchen and the living room. He said they shit all over the place. They shit in his shoe. He said he squished down into it barefoot. At night when he goes down the hall to the bathroom, he takes a flashlight to look for turds. Said he learned to do that the hard way. He was desperate to escape, even for a little while, and so when I said I'd fly him to Atlanta to see me, he asked, "How soon can I leave?"

I see him coming up the escalator at the airport. He's leaning on a cane, impossibly thin, a hundred pounds at most, a skeleton with a straggly gray-flecked beard and thin bird legs twisted somehow, crippling him in his walk. Oh no. I put my hand over my mouth to stifle myself from crying when I see how much he has deteriorated from the Razzberry I remember, in the prime of youth.

He sees me and, crying and crying, I give him a big hug. I couldn't hold back the tears after all. He tells me that it's okay. Everything is going to be okay. I feel two large bulges on his back, both the size of ping pong balls.

"They're going to cut those out," he says. "Don't worry about them, they're getting cut out."

I keep crying and holding onto him. He tells me again that everything is going to be okay. "We're back together, me and you," he says. "The Salt and Pepper Gang."

"Hell yeah." I laugh through my tears.

People are looking at us. We're a bottleneck at the top of the escalator, so I pull myself together and we get his luggage and go to the truck. His walk is all wrong even with the cane. It's like he's hobbling. He says it's because of what the stroke did to his feet. His big toes, he says, got twisted down and warped under the other toes during the stroke. There's no way of straightening them out, so he's walking with his big toes folded under, bearing the weight. It's painful. He can't use his hands the way he used to. They're like claws.

"I'm a mess," he says.

"You and me both."

We get in the truck and head south on Interstate 75 to Albany, Georgia, where I'm renting a little house to be close to my kids and my ex-wife. He marvels at the trees and how green everything is compared to Amarillo. "Tumbleweeds don't even grow in Amarillo anymore," he says. "They said forget it, man, we're out of here."

He's never been east of the Mississippi. Rose told him to be careful of the KKK and all the prejudice in the South. I tell him if anybody was ever rude to him I would go to nuclear war. Besides, Southerners are the nicest people in the world, wait and see.

He tells me about where he's living. "Man, you just don't know," he starts out. "They got fourteen dogs and four cats. None of them fixed. The cats are two males and two females. One of them is in heat if the other isn't. What I did was, I got a pack of D cell batteries and when they start up with that fighting, screaming and meowing, I throw the batteries. Rose was like, hey, what's with all these batteries all over the place? I'm like, I don't give a fuck. But the fourteen dogs, that's over the top. Every time an ambulance goes by or a loud truck, they all go to barking."

"Oh my God."

"It's bad, man. Bad! They got this rottweiler who stays by itself in the front yard because it doesn't get along with anybody. There's no grass in the front yard, nada. It's nothing but dirt and dog turds."

"They don't shovel the turds?"

"Hell no. Are you kidding me? You can't go out on the front porch to smoke a cigarette. No. The flies and the smell, forget it. You can't go in the backyard neither because that's where the rest of the damn dogs shit. Now, you want to talk about Chihuahuas?"

"Okay."

"They have five Chihuahuas. Five. All of them with bad tempers. All of them horny all of the time. None of them fixed. There's always one of them humping on some other dog, whoever is nearby, even on a damn German Shepherd that just lying there, getting humped while he's trying to sleep. I use a flyswatter on the one Chihuahua, but he keeps coming back. He's a straight up horn dog, that's all he is. He's desperate, I'm serious. I throw the batteries and I use my flyswatter on that motherfucker all day long, swear to God."

"Small dogs are not my thing."

"Chihuahuas are mean, I'm telling you. Then there's the fleas. You want to talk about fleas?"

I say yes and he tells me about the fleas.

Straightaway I know the best thing for us to do is to go fishing since we haven't fished together in over twenty-five years. We pack up my camping and fishing gear and tie my little boat on top of the truck and head out to Paradise Public Fishing Area, a campground near Enigma, Georgia that's managed by the Department of Natural Resources. It's the middle of the week, so we have the place to ourselves. We set up the tents and then tool around in the boat fishing and laughing and drinking beer.

I want to know what all happened at Anderson Dorm after I left, during his high school years. He says he was a big timer in Future Farmers of America, that he won all kinds of awards for steers and pigs at livestock shows: San Antonio, San Angelo, El Paso, Dallas, all over the panhandle, and the big Houston Livestock Show at the Astrodome, where he got sick on beer and Skoal and ran out of the Dolly Parton concert to puke in a bush. That's all fine and good, but what I want to hear are stories about what went on with all my Boys Ranch buddies, who all ran away, who got caught, who got in trouble, that kind of stuff.

We're not catching anything, not getting any bites. We reel in our lines. I fire up the trolling motor and head toward a tiny island in the middle of the lake where we tie the boat to a tree limb that gives us some shade. He tells me that during his senior year, long after Mr. and Mrs. Little left and they had new dorm parents, the Dillinghams, guys would sneak into the dorm parents' apartment when they were away and take beer out of their refrigerator. They would crawl in through the bathroom window. He says that Virgil Harbor, one of my little buddies back then, a talented criminal in elementary school, later figured out how to open their front door with a piece of wire.

I say, "No way," but that's really just to keep him going, which he does.

One time, Razzberry says, he came back drunk from a town trip to Amarillo and they undressed him in the big room at the same pool table where the ill-fated bag of Starburst once sat and you could hear cans of snuff drop out of his letter jacket. Mr. Dillingham confiscated all of it, but later they sent Virgil through his bathroom window and got it all back.

"This is exactly the kind of thing I'm interested in," I tell him.

"Oh, okay," he says. "So let's talk about Randy Earle."

"Yes! Whatever happened to Randy Earle?" Randy was this muscle-bound kid in our class and in our dorm. I used to play like I was hiding on my top bunk and he would pretend not to notice and then I would jump down on him like a wrestler. He would fall down and we'd pretend to fight in slow motion where he always let me get the best of him since I was so tiny compared to his massiveness.

"He joined the Marines," Razzberry tell me. "But listen, one time during our senior year, Randy brought back some weed from a town trip. Me and him were supposed to be cleaning out pens at the steer barn, but we smoked some of the weed and so we ended up sitting in a corner of one of the pens laughing so hard we couldn't stop. I don't even know what the hell we were laughing about but we were in tears, you know. You know, the more you try to stifle it, the worse it gets. We were late to supper at the dining hall."

"You went to the dining hall that stoned?"

"Yes. And check this out, we didn't really know that smoking pot would make you so hungry. We're at the table, scarfing down food like you never saw, everybody eyeballing us. Randy Earle couldn't stop eating. Everybody else in the whole dining hall, all four hundred people, all finished and left but we're still there, just the guys at our table because we can only leave when we're all done, remember, when the dorm parent excuses us. He was pissed off sitting there watching us, Dillingham. I think he knew something was up. How could he not? The bloodshot eyes, the giggling, the food all over our faces. I mean, come on."

"Oh my God."

"You better have some food around if Randy Earle smokes any pot, that's all I'm saying. One time, me and him on a senior weekend went to Ty and Shawn Lightfoot's sister's house. We got blasted smoking pot. Randy got all hungry but there was nothing to eat. That motherfucker goes to the refrigerator and brings back frozen corn tortillas and eats them on the couch."

"Jesus."

"So get this. Me and Randy were into huffing gas during our

senior year."

"Are you out of your mind?"

"I'm serious."

"Why? What does huffing gas do for you?"

"It fucks you up. Squares like you wouldn't know."

"I'm not that square."

"You were."

"Okay, maybe. Yes. Go on."

"So me and Randy would siphon gas out of old tractors and vehicles up at the agriculture building, and we put the gas in heavy-duty plastic see-through gloves that they used for inseminating cows and boars. That's what we'd huff out of, the glove. There was a box of them in Mr. Merle's office."

"You're demented."

"Yeah. So me and Randy go on top of one of the silos that we were supposed to be painting, and we sit up there and huff off the glove. We get so fucked up we just laugh and laugh, not noticing this staff member standing below us, looking up, listening to everything we're saying. We were so messed up, we couldn't come down the ladder. It took two or three staff to get us down."

"Did they bust your ass?"

"Hell yeah, they busted us big time.

I laugh. "I should've been there to keep you guys on the straight and narrow."

"Not possible. We were bad. Listen to this. I had some gasoline in one of them gloves and I was at the farrowing barn when everybody else left. Behind the farrowing barn, remember, they had this small cesspool for when you wash out all the pig shit. That's where I was. I go out the back and huff on the gas in the glove. I hear this wah

wah wah sound pounding in my ears and next thing you know, I step off into the cesspool and have shit up to my knees. Have to crawl out."

Back at camp, he gets a fire going and we cook steaks and drink more beer. He's got more to say about the dogs and cats at Rose's and the traumatic stress they give him, but I tell him to hold up because I want to know who Rose is and how he came to live there. So we sit in lawn chairs around the fire and he gives me some back story.

He tells me he had been working, along with his twenty-year-old son, Christopher, at a landscaping company in Amarillo with Rose's husband Phil. One day he started walking funny and Christopher pointed out to him that something looked wrong with his left leg. It was dragging. He figured he pulled a muscle or something. The next morning, he woke up with his entire left side locked down. His neck muscles didn't work, so his head dangled to the left and he couldn't move his left arm, fingers, or legs, nothing on that side. Both his big toes were warped under the other toes. He'd had a stroke in the night.

Christopher and Phil found him. They carried him to the truck and took him to the emergency room. When they got him a wheelchair in the waiting room, they said they had to go to work and so they left him there. His head started drooping to the left, but there wasn't anything he could do about it. When the nurse called his name, his voice, weakened by the stroke, wasn't loud enough for him to communicate to them that he was sitting there. He called out for help and they finally came over and took him back to a room and gave him a gown. He couldn't dress himself, so the nurse said she would go find someone to help him put on the gown. In the hospital room he started sliding down in the wheelchair, slumping and falling to the left. He called out for help, but no one could hear him. After a long time, two orderlies came into the room and picked him up and put the gown on him.

Nothing on the left side would work. The doctor came in and made some quick determinations. He got hooked up to an IV and had drugs in him and x-rays taken. They told him they would do their best, but he had to have surgery right away, right now. They operated, going in through the front of his neck under the chin to install a metal prong to pull up one spinal disc and another prong to pull the one below it down to separate them, because that was one of the root causes of his hemiparesis, or paralysis of one side of the body. The doctor said that if they had waited one more day to operate, he would likely have been permanently paralyzed.

Days and days went by in the hospital as he recovered from surgery and no one ever came to see him, except Kim Reeves of the Boys Ranch Town Office in Amarillo. A week went by.

When he gets to this part of the story, he breaks down as he tells how he cried in the hospital bed. It seemed like everyone had deserted him. No one cared that this happened to him. No one called. Nobody had any use for him anymore and never would again because how could he work in his new condition? After a week he was able to shuffle along and walk a little bit, but there was no way he could do the landscaping or construction work or hanging iron like he'd been doing. All was lost. All was hopeless.

When the hospital was ready to discharge him, he had no money, no ride, nowhere to go, no place to live, zero. He was on the streets a time or two, homeless, having to stay at the Salvation Army or the Amarillo City Mission, but that was before. How could he do that now in his condition? Phil's wife, Rose, came and saved him. She showed up on the day he was being discharged with nowhere to go and said he could live at her place.

I don't want to end the night around the campfire on such a sad, depressing note, so I tell him, "I'm going to put on some music." I go to my truck and look through my CDs. Through the windshield, I spot him hobbling out of camp to the road without his cane and I yell out, "Where are you going?"

"Come look!"

I go after him. He's going down the dark dirt road following a firefly.

"See it?"

"Yeah."

"I haven't seen a firefly since we were at Boys Ranch when we were kids," he calls back. "Come on."

The firefly cruises along in front of us at eye level, right down the middle of the dirt road, flashing its light every now and again as we follow.

"Remember the fireflies over at Cheyenne and Magenta and down by the river?" he asks.

"Yeah."

"I've never seen one since. It means something."

"You think?"

"It's leading us somewhere. Come on."

The road empties out to a large field with pine trees spaced apart like columns in a cathedral. The firefly is headed toward a swarm of other fireflies, dozens and dozens of them congregating in the pines. Razzberry is overjoyed and starts hobbling as fast as he can to join them. He goes under the pines where he stands in the middle of the blinking firefly host. It sounds like he's crying.

Something magical is happening.

Chapter Eleven

We have been sitting long enough, looking out over the lake and up at the stars, talking, and finally have to leave the cathedral of the fireflies in the pines and head back to camp. Earlier, Razzberry chased the firefly down here without his cane, and so I hold onto him and help him along. It is becoming clear to me now that he is broken not just in body, but in spirit. He has been living on a friend's couch, no way to ever work again, with absolutely nothing except his clothes, and he feels deserted by almost everyone he ever knew. I don't like seeing him cry.

My gears start turning. What he needs, I begin to think, is a music festival. When Jay and Jerry died, I went to one on the Suwanee River and camped out for three days with several thousand hippies and bohemians. I saw bluegrass, zydeco, and Americana bands on the stages they had set up under towering pines and oaks dripping curtains of Spanish moss. The music helped heal me, especially seeing it live and up close. The quote from Berthold Auerbach rang true: "Music washes away from the soul the dust of everyday life." It was the festival atmosphere itself, though, that worked as the main healing force: the smiling faces, the people dancing, children whizzing by on bicycles, campsites with folks sitting around the fire playing banjos, guitars, and fiddles. For me, it was a transformative and almost mystical experience. Hopefully, taking Razzberry to a music festival will help him the way it has helped me.

Two days later we're at Uphonia music festival, outside of Tallahassee, Florida. I'm sitting in a lawn chair at our campsite, drinking a beer, all sweaty from a million-mile walk to get ice for the cooler. Razzberry comes back from the port-a-potties, hobbling along on his cane.

"I think we're screwed," he tells me.

"Why?"

"I heard they're putting up a drum circle right over there." He points to a giant oak tree about sixty yards away.

I unwrap a piece of chocolate from a tin-foil wrapper and put it into my mouth. "I have ear plugs, so I'm not worried."

He sits in the chair beside me and holds his hand out for a piece of chocolate.

"Sorry, it was the only one. Some dude came by and gave it to me."

He reaches over and gets a beer from the cooler. "Willy Wonka?"

"A fat dude with corduroy pants made out of patches. God, this tastes like shit." I take a swig of beer to wash down the chocolate.

"Is it a mushroom chocolate?"

"A truffle? I don't think so. This tastes nasty."

"I'm talking about psychedelic."

We look at each other for a long time. His eyes get wide and he says, "Let me see the wrapper." He looks at the foil. "Did it taste like mushrooms ground up in it?"

"I don't think so. It just tasted horrible."

"It ain't no store-bought piece of candy wrapped like that."

"No. He'd have said something."

"What did he say when you got it?"

"He said, 'Hey, man, do you want a chocolate?' I said sure. He said, 'Here you go.'"

"He didn't charge you any money?"

"No."

"You ever done mushrooms before?"

"Uh, no!"

"First time for everything."

"No, because you're right, he would have charged money if it was."

"He gave it to you for free."

"Oh, please."

"We'll find out one way or the other here shortly," he says, pointing and giggling. "I'm gonna get you through this, brother. Don't you worry."

"What, are you some expert?"

"Pretty much."

An hour later I feel gross, like something is going on in my stomach. My head feels cloudy. My brain is buzzing and vibrating. Razzberry tells me that it's normal. He's so happy with himself for being right, but also, I suspect, that this is happening to me. I feel like I need to lie down in my tent but it's a thousand degrees in there. He says the best thing to do is walk it off. The crappy feeling will go away, he assures me. It's just part of the onset of the magic mushrooms.

I carry a lawn chair for Razzberry and we go down to the stages and behold the multitude of hippies assembled there. Pretty girls wearing self-made crowns of green leafy vines and little white flowers dance in the twilight. Hula hoopers hula hoop. A young mother goes after a baby running naked on the grass. People lounge about on blankets and stand around in clots grooving to the music and smoking pot. We find a spot and set up Razzberry's lawn chair. I sit on the ground beside him and hold onto his chair because the mushrooms are really kicking in. Nausea. Disorientation. I see fractal patterns behind my eyelids that morph into a wormhole. It's better if I keep my eyes open.

Another band takes the stage. Some guy is down on his haunches talking to Razzberry. Where did he come from? Is he a cop? Is he talking about me? No, he's talking about the band, the Codetalkers, on stage tuning their instruments. He points to one of the guitar players and tells Razzberry that it's Colonel Bruce. I try to focus. The four guys in the band all wear suits and ties and white shirts, but this Colonel Bruce the guy is pointing at is disheveled with his tie way too fat and short, his shirt tail untucked on one side, his hair sticking up like he just got out of bed, plus he's wearing white socks with black shoes. I try to hear what the guy is telling Razzberry about this Colonel Bruce. One of his first bands, the guy says, was back in the sixties, called the Hampton Grease Band. They put out their first album and *Spin* magazine called it one of the top five records to commit suicide to. He says that one time, they opened up for Three Dog Night and played all Three Dog Night songs. They were run off the stage and had to get a police escort to get the hell out of there. Another time he says they opened for Frank Zappa and caused a riot from the audience. He kicked Glenn Phillips in the chest and made him go flying into the speakers. Razzberry doesn't inquire who Glenn Phillips is. I sure as hell don't know.

The band starts and the guy with the encyclopedic knowledge of the guitar player sashays away into the crowd. The world behind me, out of the corner of my eye, seems to physically melt. I hold onto Razzberry's lawn chair, thinking if I turn around and look, all I will see is a deep fiery chasm and lava down below. When I close my eyes, I'm back in a kaleidoscopic whirlpool. I tell Razzberry I need to stand up and walk around. The air is hot and dense. It feels like I'm swimming through it as I make my way toward a squadron of glowing hula hoops and the mesmerizing trails of colored light that follow them.

Starting to feel giddy, I go wandering away from the crowd so people aren't looking at me. I'm being given secret information about the universe. Little elves. Subatomic. They run the whole cosmic show on a quantum physics level. I sit on the grass away from everyone. If people come too close, they will see I'm a toad now. I'm a fat, ugly water plopper. I close my eyes and I'm back to watching fractal patterns and little elves marching in rows. Or are they tiny aliens? I don't want to look at them anymore because they're scaring me, and so I go back toward the music stage and weave through the crowd to get down front. Colonel Bruce leaves his microphone stand and goes to the guy playing the stand-up bass, bends down, and takes the guy's shoe off. He holds it up to his ear like Maxwell Smart's shoe phone. I retreat into the crowd and go to the back, past the dancers and the hula hoopers, and find a spot to lie down on. I'm stretched out spread eagle looking up at the stars while Colonel Bruce sings about outer space and UFOs, and a dude comes along—doesn't see me lying there in the dark—and steps on me, planting his foot right on my nards. Full body weight. My scream goes straight up into the Milky Way.

I find Razzberry smoking a doobie at another stage and watching Keller Williams, a one-man band who loops and overdubs several guitars at blinding speed. The music is too loud, so I go stand on the

side of the huge speaker that is blasting this side of the crowd. My
attention goes to a psychedelic light show that is being projected
onto the side of a long tobacco barn. After a while I become aware of
what Keller Williams is singing into the microphone. It's something
about a freaker by the speaker. I think, no, I mis-heard that. It's the
shrooms. He sings the words again, that there's a freaker right by the
speaker. Oh my God. It's about me. I am the freaker. I forgot I was
a toad. Everybody's looking at me. I walk away from the speaker
and head back to camp, where I crawl into my tent and zip up the
flap. In the tent, I become less and less me. What was me dissolves
and I'm the witness, but now the witness dissolves and everything
is all one thing, including me if there was a me.

Sometime later, Razzberry shakes my tent and asks if I'm in
there. I grunt because there is no way I can speak any words. He
asks if I'm okay. I grunt again. He tells me to drink some water.
The drum circle starts up. I put in the ear plugs, but they do a piss
poor job of muting the torture.

The next morning, I cannot get the zipper on the tent flap to
work. It will only go up about ten inches off the ground and so I go
headfirst through the opening and wriggle out like a baby being born.
Razzberry watches, amused. "Woah, you look rough," he tells me.

I take several long gulps of water out of a jug and pour the rest
over my head. After swishing mouthwash and applying deodorant
to my pits, we go for a morning walkabout and pass by the smoky
remains of the fire at the deserted drum circle. Somebody left their
bongo drum set under the oak tree. I charge toward it.

"Oh, they're sleeping now, are they? Let me help them." I grab
the bongos and start beating on one of the drums. Razzberry comes
over and bangs on the other one. We go with an Indian chant. "Hey

ya hey ya hey ya hey. Hey ya hey ya hey ya hey." The fun lasts for about two minutes until we put down the bongos and take off to look for coffee at the vendors down by the stages.

The coffee is shitty. We dump it out and go walking down a dirt road through the pines where lots of people are camped. He wants to know about my mushroom trip, but I tell him I have no way of putting any of it into words. All I can say is that I feel really dumb for doing something so stupid. Taking candy from a stranger. Being so naive.

He tries to make me feel better by telling me that he's done things way dumber.

I ask, "Like what?"

"Like the time I joined the Navy."

"What? You?" I'm flabbergasted.

He says, "Get this," and tells me the story.

When he graduates and leaves Boys Ranch in 1980, he has a scholarship and is to start Clarendon Junior College in the fall, wanting to be a veterinarian. But, he says, he goes wild the minute he takes off his graduation gown. Spends the summer partying with ex-Boys Ranchers, drinking Southern Comfort and Wild Turkey, puking on rugs, brawling in bars, and getting thrown out of doors headfirst.

He works for a construction company hanging iron that summer, and then bails out of Clarendon Junior College after one semester and takes a farmhand job at Boys Ranch, living in one of the old bunkhouses on the far side of the ranch at Magenta. That doesn't last long. He takes off hitchhiking down to Galveston, where he parties until he runs out of money, and then hitchhikes back to Amarillo, where he meets up with Randy Earle. In town on vacation from the Marines, Randy tells Razzberry that what he needs to do is join the military. You'll learn a skill. Travel all over the world. Get good pay.

In no time he's down at the recruiting office signing on the dotted line and is enlisted into the United States Navy. They give him a first-class airline ticket to Chicago in the dead of winter. He gets hammered drunk on the plane. Around midnight, at O'Hare airport, he boards a military bus headed for the Great Lakes Naval Training Station north of Chicago near Waukegan, Illinois. When the bus pulls away from the curb, a mustachioed Chief Petty Officer stands up at the front of the bus and starts screaming bloody murder at them.

"We own your asses now, maggots! You belong to the Navy. Do you hear me?"

The recruits on the bus in unison say, "Yes, sir!" except for Razzberry, who sinks down into his seat thinking, *What the hell have I gotten myself into?*

The CPO screams again, the veins in his neck look ready to burst. "Who do you belong to?"

"The Navy, sir."

"Who?" His head is about to explode.

The boys on the bus reply louder, "The Navy, sir!"

"You will become men," The CPO says, walking down the aisle and giving them all a stink eye filled with rage. "You will become the embodiment of the Navy, do you hear me?"

"Yes, sir!"

"Do I have your attention, maggots?"

"Yes, sir!"

Well, this ain't going to work, Razzberry thinks. He's screwed up royally and he knows it. A plan starts to form in his rapidly sobering brain. When they arrive at the Naval base and get off the bus in the ice and snow, the CPO and other heinous CPOs that come out of the woodwork all get in everybody's faces and go to screaming. They march Razzberry and the other recruits into their barracks and continue shouting at them until they let them get some sleep around 2 a.m. Three hours later, the CPOs turn on the lights and rant and rave while banging on metal trash barrels they are carrying. The recruits all pop out of bed and obey the order to put their toes on the line in front of their lockers and stand at attention. All except for Razzberry. He sees what's going on and puts his head back down on his pillow and pulls the covers over himself. Two CPOs rush over to his bunk and stand on either side of him screaming at the top of their lungs and banging on the trash barrels.

"Get your ass up now, recruit! Now!"

Razzberry looks up from his pillow and says to them, "What the fuck do you want?"

Enraged, they rip the blanket and sheet off of him.

He sits on the side of the bed in his whitey tighty underwear. "What is your problem?" he asks.

Now both men stand in front of him and lean down to scream in his face. "Toes on the line! Now! Now!"

"Why?"

"Get your toes on the line and stand at attention . . . right . . . NOW!"

"Why?"

"Okay, get down and give me twenty."

"Huh?"

"Get down and give me twenty."

"That's not happening." He stands up and stretches.

"Put your toes on the damn line."

He shrugs and slowly takes his place on the line beside twenty recruits and across from twenty more who face him, all standing at attention in their underwear. One of the CPOs shouts instructions to the company of recruits about his expectations on how they will make their beds to precise military standards. Razzberry decides to pet an invisible dog. The CPOs lose their minds and run over to him and scream on either side of his face two inches away.

When they finally stop their vicious tirade to catch their breath, Razzberry says, "You're scaring my dog," and goes back to petting it. They tell him to get dressed and report to the Company Commander.

When he gets there, a guard stops him and says, "You can't come on the quarterdeck without permission."

"OK, fine."

"But you're standing on it. Go back, face the flag, then turn and ask permission to enter the quarterdeck."

"I'm already here," Razzberry says, continuing to cross the quarterdeck to a brass bell mounted on the wall. He rings it four times.

"Stop!" the guard says. "What are you doing?"

"Giving angels their wings."

The Company Commander rushes out of his office and chews Razzberry out as he pets his imaginary dog. He's sent back to re-join the recruits because the Company Commander says he knows what Razzberry is up to and is going to break him and turn him into a sailor. Razzberry gets a military buzz cut, is issued uniforms, and has to march along with the others to the chow hall. He only swings one arm when he marches; the other one is held rigidly out as if he has a dog on a leash. During physical training, he refuses to run or do push-ups or anything.

Defeated, the Company Commander tells him, "You don't belong in our Navy." Razzberry replies, "No shit." A guard escorts him to the base psychiatrist. From there, he's bustled over to a new barracks with people getting out of the Navy. He doesn't have to do anything but wait until the paperwork is processed and he's given a Section Eight discharge for being unfit for military service due to psychological problems. After collecting paychecks for another month, he is finally cut loose and flies back to Amarillo, cussing Randy Earle all the way.

I stare at him with open-mouthed disbelief but finally manage to produce words and say, "Are you out of your mind?"

He shrugs and says, "Hey, I had to do what I had to do."

Oh my God. We pick blackberries along the dirt road as campers stir and emerge from their tents zombified. He regales me with stories of depravity like how he and his buddies would drive around Amarillo and walk up into people's big backyard parties and drink their liquor until they were found out to be total strangers that nobody knew. Most of the time they fought their way out and back to their cars. Bar fights, car crashes, waking up on strange front lawns, and tales of Boys Ranchers gone wild.

We circle around to the stages, drawn by a beautiful song coming through the trees and a female singer whose voice sounds like a weary angel. Razzberry goes and asks a lady standing nearby if she knows the singer's name. It's Rebekah Pulley. I get his attention and point to the sky at paragliders landing in the open field in front of us, but he is smitten by the singer.

When I come back from breaking down camp and packing everything into the truck, Rebekah Pulley has finished playing and the stage is bare. Everyone has gone over to the second stage except for Razzberry, who sits on the ground alone.

"Hey," I call out as I walk up on him. "What's the matter with you? Why are you crying?"

He wipes his eyes with his shirt and looks away. I sit with him in silence and just let it be.

A teenager runs after a Frisbee. Ladies in sarongs and big floppy hats go by with their drinks. An old man in a tie-dye shirt pauses to look at his music schedule and then eyes the choices being offered by the food vendors.

At long last Razzberry says, "All this life you see . . ."

"Yeah?"

"It's over for me."

"What are you talking about?"

"I'm never going to do this no more, go places, go anyplace on my own. I'm never going to run again or walk without a cane. Then comes the wheelchair. They say this will only get worse."

"Don't think like that."

"I'll never drive a car again. They said no more driver's licenses for me. Can't work. How am I supposed to live? When I go back, back to Rose's and those fourteen damn dogs and the cats all in heat, I'm never going to live life no more."

"Oh, stop it."

"Why, Ken? Why did this happen to me?"

He wipes his eyes again with his shirt. I sit silently with him until he's ready to talk. In a quaking, trembling voice that kills me and makes me want to cry, he says, "Why, man? It's just not fair."

It is a full minute before I can get my emotions under control and respond. I tell him, "Do you know what Mr. Price told me one time?" He shakes his head and wipes his nose. "I was so brokenhearted about being sent to Boys Ranch. Couldn't understand why. I was a good kid. I made straight A's. Couldn't figure out what I did to deserve being sent to there, why this happened to me."

For the first time since I came back from breaking down camp and found him sitting on the ground, he looks me in the eyes.

"I was a mama's boy," I tell him. "Playing with toys, watching cartoons, shielded from the world. I had no idea that bad things happened, no notion that violence and disease and tragedy are visited on everybody at one time or another. Me getting sent to Boys Ranch was a shock and it was unfair, I thought. One day Mr. Price woke me up to the fact that I wasn't the only one, that misfortune and problems are part and parcel of life, no way around it. There would never be an answer to 'Why me?' because bad things happen, and sometimes a bad thing, later on down the line, turns out to not be bad at all, even though at the time you wouldn't have known it. Price was right as rain. Looking back, being sent to Boys Ranch was the best thing that could have happened to me. I know that now."

"Me, too."

"Like when my daughter got diagnosed with autism. I didn't take it well, at all. How could God do this to her? Why? First I turned to tequila, then to TV preachers who promised miracles, but autism wasn't going to just go away. Luckily I came across a book that echoed what Mr. Price had said to me back then. Joseph Campbell was the author. Half of the books on my bookshelf at the house are by him. He was an expert scholar on world mythologies."

"Never heard of him."

"Anyway, here I was, evidently thinking that suffering was for everybody else, not me, not my family. We're exempt. Disease, death, being a victim of crime, autism, all that happened to other people, right? No. So foolish for me to be royally upset, as if God is intentionally punishing me and her. All life is going to involve sorrow at some point. At many points. Looking back, I'm now glad the cosmos got me to be her father, to be the one there for her as she goes through life. There's no 'Why me?' anymore. Like Price said, there might not be a reason, but there might be a lesson."

The next day, back at my house, I call his attention to my bookshelf, telling him that the books I've got are the books I'm going to keep with me the rest of my life. *The Perennial Philosophy* and *Heaven and Hell*, both by Aldous Huxley. *Man's Search for Meaning* by Viktor Frankl. *The Journey to the East* and *Siddhartha* both by Hermann Hesse. Frazer's *The Golden Bough*. James Joyce's *The Portrait of the Artist as a Young Man*. Everything by Tolkien. Several books by Alan Watts, especially *The Way of Zen*. Thoreau's *Walden* and *Letters to a Spiritual Seeker*. *The Essential Jung*, edited by Joseph Campbell. "Self-Reliance," by Ralph Waldo Emerson. *The Upanishads*. Many works by Joseph Campbell including *The Hero With a Thousand Faces* and *Myths to Live By*. I also show him the books by G.A. Henty that Mr. Seymour gave me at Boys Ranch when he had his eye on molesting me.

I take ahold of one of the books and flip through it to show him a passage. It's *The Hero Within* by Carol Pearson. I tell him that she describes me before I went to Boys Ranch with her archetype of "The Innocent," and me after I got to the ranch with her archetype of "The Orphan." She explains the process of going from the innocent to the orphan. I read him the passage: "Before the journey, the Innocent lives in an unfallen world, a green Eden where life is

sweet and all one's needs are met in an atmosphere of care and love."
That describes me on the day before I went to Boy's Ranch. Then
comes the fall. Pearson gives the example of David Copperfield in
an orphanage. This fall, as she puts it, is from innocence and beauty
into a realization that the world is full of disappointment and pain.
It is the first lesson.

The interesting thing, I tell Razzberry, is that she describes the
process of going from innocent to orphan as "the fortunate fall."
The kind of thing you think is bad, but later you realize was what
you needed. I grab one of Joseph Campbell's books that I've heavily
earmarked, *The Inner Reaches of Outer Space*, and tell him about
something Schopenhauer had written, called "A Transcendent Spec-
ulation upon an Apparent Intention in the Fate of an Individual."
Campbell captured Schopenhauer's thesis, and I read it aloud to
Razzberry: "In the later years of a lifetime, looking back over the
course of one's days, one notices how encounters and events that
appeared at the time to be accidental became the crucial structuring
features of an unintended life story through which the potentialities
of one's character were fostered to fulfillment."

"What we need to do," I tell him, "is to see if we can discover
what the lesson is for you."

"I guess I'll think about it when I go back, if those damn dogs
give me a minute."

"Let's change your airline ticket."

"What?"

"I think you should extend your stay a little while. The Salt and
Pepper Gang hasn't really gotten going yet in my opinion. You ever
been to North Carolina?"

"No."

"Want to go? There's a music festival next weekend." His eyes get wide and a big grin takes over his face. I tell him, "Saddle up."

Chapter Twelve

North of Atlanta as we drive to Asheville, where we'll be going to another music festival, Razzberry asks me if I want to hear a story that will blow my mind. He wants to tell me the next chapter of his history. I don't know how it could be any more shocking than using an imaginary dog to get out of the Navy, but I'm all ears.

He tells me that after the fiasco of the Navy, he is determined to make better choices in life, but not yet, and so when he arrives back in the dustbowl of Amarillo, Texas, with three or four un-cashed paychecks, he meets up with all his old buddies and they buy a lot of beer and booze and pot. He sees ZZ Top, Nazareth, Lover Boy, Cheap Trick, and all the bands that come through Amarillo. When the partying dies down, he hitchhikes from Amarillo to Galveston, where a buddy said he could get him a job, but that doesn't work out so he thumbs his way back up to the very top of Texas, to Perryton, right on the Oklahoma border. An ex–Boys Rancher buddy gets him a job hanging steel during the construction of a Wesco Oil facility.

He's bored as hell in Perryton. It's all oil and gas land or it's ranch land with hundreds of head of cattle or it's farmland. No matter what, the landscape is flat all the way to the horizon: corn, soybeans, sorghum, and especially wheat. There's not much to do in Perryton after work, except hang out in the bar and shoot pool and listen to the jukebox, but Razzberry tells me he's figured out how to make the tiny town bearable and how to find happiness in the situation. It involves three things: Quaaludes, marijuana, and booze. This is in the early eighties right before Quaaludes were outlawed. Taking them made you mellow out, especially when you threw in some alcohol. If you couldn't score any Quaaludes, then smoking a big fat doobie put you in a happy frame of mind, no problem.

His buddies at work introduce him to a girl from Kansas who can get him a quarter of a pound of pot if he wants it. He does. That could last for months. If he gets that, there will be no need to incur the constant risks involved in driving long distances to try to score small amounts. Pot isn't easy to come by in those days, especially in a tiny town way up in the Texas Panhandle. Get it wholesale, that's the smart way to go, he thinks.

What he does next is decidedly not smart, and there's no way of excusing it, he tells me. He says that after work one day, he borrows the work truck to go pick up his quarter pound of pot, drinks a beer, and puts a little piece of purple microdot acid blotter paper under his tongue. LSD. For an hour he drives north out of Texas wondering if he got ripped off, waiting for the acid to take effect. It kicks in when he is outside of Hugoton, Kansas, headed west into the sunset. The top of his head starts tingling. He has a momentary bout of mild nausea and a clammy feeling. Trails of colored light follow his fingers when he moves his hands through what looks like a charged field of multicolored energy. The setting sun casts long, brilliant golden rays through pink and purple clouds. He's got a sudden urge to laugh, but the intensity of the feeling of joy also makes him want to cry with happiness.

The dealer, when he gets there, sees him smiling ear to ear and acting strangely. She watches Razzberry take a slow but very out-stretched step like the cartoon guy in the Keep on Truckin' poster. As she rolls them a joint, the dealer asks, "So, what are you on, Razzberry?" Unable to summon words, he just smiles and slow-motion shrugs while lifting his hands in the air. The guessing game takes one guess. "You're tripping," the dealer says.

She marvels at him, amazed, impressed, and a bit worried. She helps pack the brick of marijuana into Razzberry's Navy sea bag and sends him on his way back to Perryton. By then it is dark and the hallucinations come on strong. The white dotted lines on the highway float up and zoom through the cab next to Razzberry's head. His hands are fixed at ten and two on the wheel. Somehow he makes it back to his motel room. He spends the rest of the night hallucinating and walking around outside looking at the sky.

When it is time to go to work the next morning, he is still awake and the acid is starting to wear off. He rides to work with a buddy named Jesus. He tells him about getting the pot and that he has been tripping on acid all night long. Jesus, long haired and bearded, with the doe-like eyes of Christ, says, "Oh my God. You're a maniac."

After work, Jesus and Razzberry go back to the motel and roll up a joint, but Razzberry is too tired to smoke it. He lies down on his bed and crashes. Jesus says he wants to buy a little amount of it when Razzberry wakes up.

As Razzberry sleeps, a number of events happen at the motel. Jesus turns on the TV, smokes the joint, and watches *The A-Team*. Someone knocks. Jesus fans at the cloud of marijuana smoke heavy in the air and goes to the door. Two dudes from work stand there holding beers. Jesus motions at Razzberry lying there sleeping. The two nod and quietly enter and watch *The A-Team* while Jesus rolls another joint. During a commercial, one of the dudes leaves to go get his cooler of beer. He comes back with another dude. Whispering and giggling, they crowd into the bathroom and smoke a joint, blowing smoke out the window. They cough and laugh and try to keep quiet, but eventually see that it doesn't matter. Razzberry isn't going to wake up even if a bomb goes off. Soon they are sitting on the bed beside him, guzzling beer and yukking it up as the TV blares. They play cards and smoke cigarettes with the motel room door propped open.

Meanwhile, coming up the street, a scrawny long-haired dude named Tony, who Jesus and Razzberry knew from the bar, crosses over toward the motel. They don't know much about Tony except he is a local, a kid just out of Perryton high school, probably living with his parents. As he crosses the street, Tony gives a nod to an officer in an Ochiltree County Sheriff's car at the Dairy Queen next to the hotel. The officer nods back.

Tony goes to Razzberry's room and joins the party. After a while he persuades Jesus to sell him ten dollars' worth of pot out of Razzberry's stash. Jesus doesn't think Razzberry would mind. Tony pays his ten bucks, his eye on Razzberry's sea bag that Jesus had gone into to get the weed. He then leaves and on his way down the street, gives a thumbs up sign to the Ochiltree County Sheriff's officer at the Dairy Queen.

Shortly afterwards, Razzberry feels he's being shaken. People are telling him to get up. Cops stand over him saying, "Get up, boy." They grab him and haul him out of bed and put him against the wall. They point at the bag of pot on the table and ask if that belongs to him. Jesus stands against the wall with his hands up and denies that the bag is his. Six or seven cops and deputies crowd the room, poking through everything. One of them pulls out the brick of marijuana from the sea bag. Razzberry takes the rap.

The cop who puts the cuffs on him is a real jerk. He says, "You ain't gonna bring your black ass up into my town selling pot."

"I wasn't selling anything!"

"Tell it to the judge."

The cops take Jesus and two other card players to jail, but Razzberry is the one that has bail set too high for him or any of his friends to pay. He's stuck in the Ochiltree County jail for six weeks.

In there with him for most of the duration is an enormous biker with a long beard. They hit it off and become buddies, laughing and kidding around non-stop. The jailer's wife brings them home-cooked meals and board games from her house. They watch TV in the day room and get hooked on a soap opera, *Guiding Light*. Missing an episode is unthinkable. Diane is trying to get Alan to remove Phillip from his will. Justin and Jackie Marler are Phillip's biological parents and so he's not a Spaulding, is he? That's how Diane is probably going to try to blackmail Alan; she's found out. Plus, she's now going after Harry and Vanessa. Razzberry and the biker discuss *Guiding Light* all through the days. They announce theories and offer up guesses on what will happen next.

The jailer tells Razzberry one day that his court-appointed lawyer is here, a man with a huge gray cowboy hat and smoking a cigar. He says, "Boy, I'm going to do as good as I can for you," and tells him that he's been bailed out by his old boss at the construction company and gives him his court date. When the lawyer calls him "boy" he knows he is screwed.

He sleeps on a friend's couch for a couple of days with the thought of going to prison weighing on his mind. One day he gets up, takes his backpack, and goes walking down the highway with this thumb out. He's decided to skip his court date and go roaming through Texas, headed south.

We pull into Deerfields, North Carolina at Smilefest to get our tickets. I tell him, "Yeah, this is blowing my mind. More than the imaginary dog." At the ticket shack standing in line, I keep my voice low and say to him, "You mean to tell me that you were going to drive two hours north to Kansas to buy a huge amount of pot and you said to yourself, 'You know what? I should drop acid before I head out.' What kind of person thinks like that?"

"Razzberry," he answers matter-of-factly.

"Oh my God. I hope Mr. Price doesn't know any of this."

"He might know a little."

When we get our tickets, we drive through apple orchards and dogwood trees down into a valley with two lakes at the bottom and set up our tents under huge shade trees by the stream coming down from the mountains. He's having a hard time moving his left leg, slinging it forward and using his cane, and I'm having to pick him up when he falls and stay close by his side as we go along through the campground to the music stages and vendors. I usually catch him when he trips over a root or a tent stake, but sometimes he goes down hard and everybody is aghast. They're probably thinking he's drunk or on drugs, but he's not. I wish I could let everybody know that he is doing the best he can and to stop staring at us. If he'd just listen to me and rest every so often and not wear himself out, it would be easier. But he's Razzberry, he says, and he's going to be what he's going to be. I like that actually, meaning I am the enabler. In my mind, my job is to let him experience as much life and music and beauty as possible before he goes back to Amarillo and the menagerie of animals in Rose's trailer. I'm getting more and more worried about what will happen to him when he goes back. The good thing is that he's got Kim Reeves at the Boys Ranch Town Office trying to get him approved for government disability and housing assistance. There it is again, I tell Razzberry, the thing I so hated at the time, Boys Ranch, proving more and more to be a gift in my life and his, like Mr. Price forecasted. He agrees.

We put our backpack of cold beers under his lawn chair at the main stage. The band is called Mood Cultivation Project and Razzberry says, "That's the project you ought to be working on, man." I stare at him until he explains. "Mood cultivation. Go find us some weed."

"I'm not going looking for weed." I hand him a beer. "Besides, how am I supposed to do that?"

"Ask around. Look at those hippies over there. Go ask them."

"No. You're out of your mind."

"I will."

"Go for it. I'm going exploring. I'll be back."

I take off and scout out the other stage over by a pond at the base of a steep incline and the mountain above. Why not hike up there a little way and look out over the land? Off I go upwards, sliding at times, holding onto vines and branches, crawling on hands and knees. There's a small patch of level ground before the next major inclination. It's a tiny meadow with flowers. I stop and declare victory because I'm all out of breath. The thought occurs to me to twirl around with outstretched arms like Julie Andrews and sing "The Hills Are Alive." I don't. I sometimes just think stupid thoughts.

Going back down, momentum and gravity have me picking up speed until my legs can't keep up and I tumble and roll and am lashed across the face by branches and thorns. Bleeding, disheveled, my face dirty, I walk up to Razzberry at his chair with a group of hippies he's acquired who sit at his feet smoking cigarettes. Oh, my bad, it's not cigarettes they're smoking. Razzberry has red slits for eyes.

When he sees me, he says, "Jesus!"

One of the hippies asks, "Dude, what happened?"

"Parachute didn't open," I tell them. "Landed on the mountain." All their mouths drop open. I stoically walk to the port-a-potties.

That evening, we put our backpack stuffed with beer and ice under Razzberry's chair at the main stage and go to the vendors to see what kinds of food they're offering. We settle on the gumbo. I take him to the stage by the pond, but he's having a lot of trouble getting his left leg to work and he needs to sit down and rest along the way. I see the pain written on his face and I work to get him back to his chair, holding onto him because he's having trouble going down the dirt road. People stop and ask if we're okay, and I tell them no problem. We're the Salt and Pepper Gang. He's my brother. We got this.

When we make it back to the main stage, it's crowded and we can't find his chair. It's hard to work our way through the crowd, even though people make room for him when they see him coming along with a cane. At last we locate the chair with the backpack beneath it. He takes the backpack and sits in the chair with it on his lap. Everyone around us dances to Colonel Bruce and the Codetalkers. The Colonel's hair sticks up at odd angles, his shirt is untucked, a middle button is open, white socks, black shoes; he's magnificent. We're happy to see him here. The band invites a guy named Wildman Steve to come onstage. He's a dude with long, stringy blonde hair, glasses, a colorful dashiki shirt, a shiny metal washboard, and thimbles on all ten fingers. He's crazy insane on the washboard.

Razzberry digs into the backpack and tries to hand me a can of Pabst Blue Ribbon. "Oh hell no," I say and push it away. "I want my Sam Adams."

"Fine." He opens the beer and takes a drink before digging into the backpack. "Sorry," he says, "There's no Sam Adams in here."

I don't believe him and take a look myself. "You son of a bitch. PBR? That's the shittiest of the shittiest of shitty beers. That's all you packed?"

He takes another swig, happy as a clam.

"I'm not drinking that piss brew."

"Don't blame me. I didn't pack it, you did."

I think about it for a second and realize he's right, but I put Sam Adams and Red Stripe in there. I don't think we even brought any PBR. My Spidey sense activates and I notice two enormous ladies with their arms crossed and annoyed looks on their faces standing behind me. They're flanked by two Paul Bunyanesque men glaring at us. I lean down with as much nonchalance as I can fake and say into Razzberry's ear, "Get up, we gotta go."

"Why?"

"That's not our backpack. That's not your chair. Not your beer."

"What?"

"Get your cane. Follow my lead."

We knife through the crowd and eventually locate our backpack and get wasted watching the Drive By Truckers, a southern rock band. They sing a song telling the other side of the Buford Pusser story and what a bastard he was. They sing about daddy getting shot on the front porch in front of the kids. All their songs are about living in the South, being poor and broke, trying hard but not getting anywhere in a wasteland of trailer parks and crappy job prospects. They tear into songs about killing law men, songs about droughts and floods, tornadoes and cancer, about dropping acid, drinking a fifth of vodka and throwing yourself off a mountain.

When the show's over, Razzberry's left side starts to quit on him as we lurch and lumber back to camp. He's in pain all night in his tent and makes distressed noises that worry me.

The next morning, we sit in the shade and drink the coffee I percolated on the fire. I make him pick up where he left off with his story of depravity and lawlessness in the eighties.

He starts off by telling me about the prejudice he had to endure in some of the towns up in the Texas Panhandle like Spearman, Canadian, Booker, and Perryton. Some people didn't even try to hide it like they do nowadays. He reminds me of the time he and I sat on the floor in Anderson Dorm and watched the miniseries *Roots* on TV, how we couldn't even imagine racism back then until we watched it portrayed. There wasn't any racism in our dorm. I agree with him that the black guys in Anderson Dorm were leaders and heroes: Kenny Davis, the pitcher on our softball team, a bronc rider and rattlesnake hunter; and Lonnie Wade, my room leader and State wrestler. And then there was Razzberry, who everybody loved. The thing is, we don't know what Kenny or Lonnie or any of those dudes experienced or what they saw, only what we saw. Their experience is their own. We can't know. Razzberry nods.

He goes on with his story. When he gets bailed out of jail and hitchhikes south to get out of the Texas Panhandle, he is amazed at the friendly people he runs across along the way, the ones that give him rides and feed him and take him where he wants to go, the ones that say a prayer with him when he gets out of their truck and make him take the money they're offering. So much human kindness, is how he describes it. He sleeps beneath underpasses and writes poems in a journal until he reaches a little farming town by San Angelo and looks at a corkboard in a grocery store. He pulls down the card of a local farmer who is looking for help plowing fields and working on his ranch. At the payphone outside, he plugs in a quarter and calls the man, who comes and gets him in his truck. He tells the man what he knows about farming and driving tractors, stuff he learned at Boys Ranch, and the man is surprised. He brings Razzberry to his house and introduces him to his wife. They welcome him and prepare a steak dinner for him. He loves their house with the huge fireplace, the Western-style furniture, the old halters and antique farming implements hanging on the wall, and the collection of types of barbed wire.

They get him situated in their bunkhouse out back and show him the freezer full of beef in the garage. He can pull out anything he wants and cook it on the grill at his bunkhouse. If he needs to go to town to get groceries, he can use one of the trucks. They've got hearts of gold, he says, and treat him with respect. The farmer's wife does his laundry and folds it. She makes pies and invites him down to the house all the time. He earns his money by driving tractors, plowing, moving irrigation pipes, and feeding the cattle. What he loves the most is getting on a horse and riding fences.

One day when he is out plowing, the farmer pulls up in his truck and waves him down. The farmer tells him that a man called and said he was a bounty hunter. He'd be calling back in a couple of hours. Razzberry admits the bounty hunter is after him. He finishes plowing the field and goes to the house to take the call.

"Hi, Mr. Hill," the bounty hunter says on the phone, "I want to come get you tomorrow, around mid-day. Are you going to be there?"

"Yes, sir, I'll be right here."

"Don't try running."

"Don't worry, sir. I won't."

The farmer and his wife invite him for dinner that evening. He tells them everything about Perryton and how remorseful he is that he got into trouble. They never judge him. The next day, a Mercedes Benz pulls up to the house. The bounty hunter, tall, dressed in jeans and boots and a cowboy hat, gets out. Razzberry goes to him with his hands out, wrists together.

"I'm not going to handcuff you, man," the bounty hunter says.

Razzberry hugs the farmer and his wife, both of them teary eyed.

They head north for a few hours and then get a motel room with two double beds. The bounty hunter takes him to a nice steak restaurant. The next day, he lets Razzberry drive the Mercedes while he pulls his cowboy hat over his face and takes a nap in the passenger seat.

Back in Perryton at the Ochiltree County jail, his big, cigar-chomping lawyer in the gray cowboy hat says to Razzberry, "Boy, I'm going to do the best I can for you," and Razzberry again knows he's screwed. In court, they have his quarter pound of pot sitting on the evidence table. The prosecutor points at it and asks him, "Mr. Hill, is that your marijuana?"

"Yeah."

The judge gives him two years in the state penitentiary and turns him over to the Texas Department of Corrections.

"Oh my God," I blurt out. "I hope Mr. Price doesn't know about this."

"He might know a little."

Chapter Thirteen

About an hour outside of Chattanooga, Razzberry and I start passing dozens and dozens of cars on the shoulder of the interstate. We are still twelve miles from our exit in Manchester where we have to get ice and supplies for Bonnaroo. He's talked me into taking him to one more music festival before he goes back to Texas for surgery to remove the painful lumps on his spine. He says he has started taking his medicine again. He'd stopped for a while because of how groggy and nauseated the pills make him, and he says he won't wear himself out anymore like he's been doing. I thought of renting a wheelchair for him, but it would be impractical on the dirt and gravel roads from what I read about the festival online. All these cars we're passing on the shoulder is a mystery. We're too far away for it to be Bonnaroo traffic. There must be some other event nearby, a big racetrack or something, and that's what this huge line of cars is about. That idea evaporates when we notice what's written on the back windows of cars we pass. Do You Roo? Bonnaroo or Bust. Roo 2005.

This is the line. Fifteen miles long. We keep going because the plan now is to get off the exit at Manchester, get ice and food and snacks, and then go back on the interstate the way we came and get in the long line. We pass hundreds of cars on the shoulder with each passing mile. At the Manchester exit, police stand in the road and stop us. If we're not locals, we're not allowed to go into town. The officer says there's going to be 90,000 people at Bonnaroo and if they were allowed in the tiny town, it would be total gridlock and the residents wouldn't be able to get anywhere with the whole place logjammed. He motions for us to get in the line, but if we do, we will be cutting in front of a least a thousand cars that we've passed, people that have been in that line for five hours or more. My hesitation pisses off the officer. Razzberry tells me to just do it. I have no other choice.

The universe acts quickly and delivers bad karma when we get to the entrance through a fence into an open field. The line branches off into ten lanes headed toward ten shade shelters where employees take tickets and put wristbands on people. I look around for a will call booth or tent because I purchased the tickets online. A festival worker tells me will call is two miles further up the interstate in a little town. He advises me to try to move the truck over to the fence line and walk there. We're hemmed in by a thick crush of cars behind us, so it's impossible to get back on the interstate. After we get the truck out of the way by the fence, I leave Razzberry in command and take off with a bottle of water on a five-mile-round-trip death march in ninety-degree heat.

On the interstate, cops divert cars away from the entrance we went through, and so a long queue of cars on the shoulder stretches out ahead. The exhaust I have to go through is thick and nauseating. The sun scorches me. Can't keep the sweat out of my eyes. I make it to the town. The mechanics in a tire shop let me re-fill my water bottle and stand in front of their fan. I find the will call place, a tiny building that looks abandoned with grass growing through the cracks in the sidewalk.

On my way back, trucks fly past at eighty miles an hour. Bugs and gnats swarm my face, forcing me to go along waving both hands around my face and ears like a crazy person. I stagger up, on the verge of heatstroke, and say to Razzberry, who's sitting in the shade beside the truck, "Water."

"We've got a problem," he says.

"I need water."

"That's part of the problem. We ain't got no water."

"We've got jugs and jugs of it."

"Not no more. I had to pour it out."

"What?"

"Look," he says, pointing. "See those workers in the red shirts with 'safety' on the back?"

"Yeah."

"See how they're going through everybody's shit? They're looking through everybody's coolers and confiscating anything in a glass bottle." Piles of perfectly good six packs and twelve packs of beer along with a dragon's horde of bottles of liquor sit in front of the ticket taker booths. "All we got is bottled beer, man!"

"Oh my God."

"So I've been opening these bottles and pouring them into jugs." Fifteen or twenty bottles of Red Stripe and Sam Adams are open. "I got three jugs so far. Had to dump out the water."

"All the water?"

"Yeah." He uses a bottle opener on a Sam Adams and hands it to me. Better drink up, because all this beer will never fit into the one jug I got left."

"This is even worse karma! Pouring out all our beer. Oh Jesus God."

"You shouldn't have cut in line."

"You SOB. This is worse than Starburst."

"We'll live."

We sit and drink as many beers as we can and watch people get searched and have their stuff confiscated. We climb in the truck and merge back in line. They search us and give us wristbands and escort us through fields to other workers who direct us to a camping spot five feet from the next vehicle, with only enough space behind us to pitch two tents. Immediately behind us, another row of densely packed vehicles arrives. We're pinned in for the duration.

Standing on the bed of the truck, we look out over thousands of tents of the people who got here before us, packed like sardines all the way to the horizon. Razzberry wants to know when we go to the music stages, how will we ever find our way back? We look at the map they gave us when we got our tickets and see if we can match it up to the terrain. The camping areas on the Bonnaroo map are laid out in a series of grids, each with its own name. If we figure out where we are, we can locate ourselves on the map and see the name they gave us. We see Centeroo, with the stages, way off in the distance and locate it on the map. There's no way we are in Camp Fat Bastard or Camp Mini-Me or those *Austin Powers* camps; they're across some road. Clearly we're not anywhere near Camp Pussy Galore and Camp Miss Moneypenny and the *James Bond* camps. Camps Marsellus Wallace, Vincent Vega, Zed, and the other *Pulp Fiction* areas are next to the RV camp, and we don't see RVs anywhere around us. One of our camping neighbors overhears what we're trying to figure out and tells us we're in Camp Darth Vader. A-ha. Now we have a chance of finding our way back.

Razzberry isn't feeling well. He says it's the medicine he started taking again that's the problem. All the beer he guzzled while he waited for me to get back with our tickets isn't helping. It's probably not good in combination with his pills. I help him down from the truck and get him in a chair in the shade. He watches me set up our tents and makes smart-ass remarks as I struggle and screw things up. Such a critic.

I leave him to rest up while I go on a reconnaissance mission to check out the place. Off I go and join thousands walking along the dirt road in a sea of bobbing heads like the sidewalks in New York City. Young people sit on the ground by the road passing joints and pipes as cops on Clydesdales saunter past, not caring. A guy walking by calls out, "I got your heady blue diamonds." I grab ahold of a dude and ask him what the hell is that guy talking about? He's selling Viagra. Here comes a winner, the happiest dude I've seen so far, walking past and announcing, "I got your Windows XP manual!" He holds it in the air and laughs hysterically until he can get it together and make the announcement again. The guy behind him yells out like a hotdog vendor, "Mushrooms, get your mushrooms!" A skinny older man wearing boots and only a diaper asks if I want a shot of Jägermeister. I do, but I say I don't. What about a can of Pringles for two bucks? No, thank you. Jesus, Joseph, and Mary, what is going on here? People spread out in all directions. There goes a spaceman. There goes a man wearing an oversized costume and a giant papier-mâché head of an angry Cyclops.

I'm not in Texas anymore, Zappa.

It's not that far to Centeroo, but it will be a major ordeal for Razzberry because inside, the music stages are spread out far from one another. The lines to get through security are long and everyone is searched and patted down. It's like a little town inside the security perimeter. The Ferris wheel gives it a Pleasure Island feel. They've got a cinema tent and a comedy club, a festival of beers from micro-breweries, an internet village and an arcade. There are batting cages, lots of shops and food choices, heavy foot traffic, and drugs being smoked out in the open. A girl dressed as Heidi walks past with a basket of joints, passing them out for free. She gives me one. This will make me a hero when I take it back to Razzberry.

I get to the campsite but he's not there, probably out exploring. The ice is melted because the cooler lid wasn't pushed down all the way, damn him. The beer in the jugs is flat and undrinkable. Before I go back out in the heat to get ice and beer and water, I sit in the truck and blast the air conditioning. The weatherman on the radio says rain is on the way, with much more coming behind that as tropical storm Arlene comes ashore at Pensacola and looks to travel north right on top of us, much weakened by the time it gets to Tennessee, but still a rainmaker. I need to put the rainflys over our tents. When I go to do it, I see Razzberry lying in his tent, soaked in sweat and watery vomit, convulsing with dry heaves.

"What the hell?" I go into the tent. It's like an oven in here, so I take him by the armpits and drag him out onto the grass. I take off my shirt and wipe his face, but he needs water. There's none. After I get the shade umbrella positioned over him, I tell him to hold on, and I run through the maze of tents toward Shakedown Street, where the illegal vendors squat on both sides of the dirt road. At a stand selling grilled cheese sandwiches, I buy two bottles of water and run back. He's still dealing with the dry heaves and so I get another shirt from my bag and wipe his face and neck and put a water bottle to his lips.

"Drink." I get down beside him and cradle his head in my lap. His convulsions have stopped, but he's out of it and won't take a sip. "You're dehydrated," I tell him and pour water in his mouth. He gags and coughs it out, but it gets him out of the stupor. I pour more into his mouth and it runs down his chin and onto his chest. "Do you want me to get the medics or call 911?" He makes noises and shakes his head no, gets up on an elbow, and takes the bottle of water.

What if it was the exhaust coming from the truck while I sat in the air conditioning that made him sick? His tent's only four feet away. I could've killed him. Never going to make that mistake again. I run and get my battery-operated fan and place it so that it blows on his face, and then I use a towel to clean him up. He downs the rest of the water and then I hand him the other bottle I brought.

"Are you okay?

He nods and lies back down. I get a rolled-up sleeping bag to prop his head upon, readjust the shade umbrella, and put a rag dipped in the cooler's melted ice water on his forehead. As he naps, I watch over him and pass the time reading some of the poems in his bookbag. He calls his collection of poems written over the years *Razz Mind Speaking*.

Run run Razz
Run as fast as you can
Don't look behind
Run run Razz
The lights are on you
The fishing hole has gone dry
Run run Razz

The world's closing in
No time left
Run run Razz
Hang onto your hat
The storm is on the way
Things are coming undone
It's going to get rough
So hang onto your hat Razz
Because you're falling by yourself
Nobody left but yourself
So hang onto yourself
That's all you've got

Childhood days
Wish I had them back
I need a shirt tail to hang onto
Can't I just go back
Standing by the cattails
The smell of the pond in my nose
A can of worms and a cane pole
Help me Lord my bones are burning
My brain is aching, my feet are dragging
Take me Lord to the county and the simple life
Take me back

Did you see me today?
Will you know me today?
Can you spare some change for me?
Do you have a pillow to give me?

But you're scared of me
You don't like my limp
I shake too much
You want to run away from me
I was hoping for a handout
But I'm not what you're looking for
So nobody saw me today

Hey Mr. Black man what are you doing today
And you Mr. Brown man does the world look the same
to you
Everybody thinks Mr. White man owns the world
The world belongs to all of us not just one
The world is brown and black and white and all the colors
The world belongs to God and nobody sees that
We're running around looking at each other's colors
And thinking we're better than the other colors
But no color is better than another color
When the Lord comes, color won't matter
So let's live together and not kill each other

My time runs short
My body's breaking down
When I look at myself I want to cry
My body melts away
Just skin and bones
I know I won't win
The battle with my body
Lord hear my dream

I don't want gold or silver
I want to be loved by a lady again
But a broken down man don't get love from a lady
I have no gold in my pockets
No brick castle for a house
No body at all
I feel the pain in my bones
Drugs and pills don't stop it
My steps get slower
No strength no more
I shake and shake
Slipping away
Wasting away
Guess that's how it goes
I had a good life though
When my bones ache
I go back to my childhood days
But now it's time to go
Given up on doctors
Just slipping away

Nobody told me I was dying today
Nobody told me I would die alone
And nobody told me love would kill you
That friends would turn away
I don't want nothing from you
Don't shy away from me because I walk funny
I just want you to be you
And Razz to be Razz

I got nothing to give except manners and respect
Nobody told me I'd fade away
Nobody told me I'd die today

When he wakes up, he drinks more water and eats the grilled cheese sandwich I went and got him, but he's unnaturally quiet, his face sad and gloomy. "I'm sorry, Ken," he says and wipes away a tear.

"What are you sorry for? You got nothing to be sorry about."

"I don't want to be a burden and ruin your good time, man."

"You're out of your mind. My good time is hanging out with you."

He sighs and shakes his head. "If this hadn't happened to me, we probably could have had a hell of a time."

"We are having a hell of a time. Besides, if that hadn't happened to you, you'd probably be way out of control. Probably have bounty hunters involved again."

While we're resting up in the shade before the long trek into Bonnaroo, I make him continue his story. Maybe that will help get him out of his funk.

He tells me that when the judge gives him his two-year sentence at the state penitentiary, his lawyer says to him, "Boy, I did the best I could for you." A gung-ho deputy and an older officer drive him and another prisoner to the prison south of Dallas. The deputy handcuffs them with their hands behind their backs and puts them in a squad car. After a few miles, the officer makes the deputy pull over and take off the cuffs. The deputy is pissed and says that if they run, he's going to shoot them. Annoyed, the seasoned officer tells the deputy they're not going anywhere wearing orange suits that say "prisoner" across the damn backs. They stop at a restaurant for a final meal. Razzberry hears that the deputy is a Dallas Cowboys fan and proceeds to trash talk him and Tom Landry and goes on and on about how Tony Dorsett fumbles so much and how Danny White is the worst. Razzberry asks him if he remembers all those Super Bowls where the Steelers kicked the Cowboys' asses. The more the deputy fumes, the more the older officer smiles.

Prison intake at the diagnostic center is scary. All the new prisoners are forced to strip naked and stand in a row with all the other prisoners and guards looking at them. They have to bend over and let the guards look up their butts. Fresh meat, the other prisoners call out. They issue him white prison pants and shirts. An old black barber in prison thirty years for murder gives him a buzz cut.

"This your first time in?" the barber asks.

Razzberry nods.

"I can see you're scared. Let me tell you how to do your time. You go in as a man, you act as man, and you'll come out as a man. If you roll over, you'll be a punk."

It's worrying, how many prisoners stare at him and comment like they're sexual deviants. The prison is overcrowded, and so the new arrivals sleep in big tents in the courtyard until a place can be found for them. They are put to work right away and march out from the prison gates to the fields, where all day they hoe long rows that shimmer in heat waves. They've got to hoe in time with the other prisoners as the big guard on a horse calls the cadence, "One, two, three, step. One, two, three, step." When they pass out from the heat, they're thrown onto wagons until the guards revive them, and then they're put right back on the line hoeing, shoveling, or doing whatever back-breaking work they're given.

Razzberry's first cellmate is a black dude in for armed robbery, but there are bad vibes between the two of them. So Razzberry sends in a kite, which is prison talk for a paper request, to get moved to a different cell and they put him on the third floor with an eighteen-year-old white kid named Hobart, in for grand theft auto. Hobart shows him how to make a shank by using razors to slice down the end of a toothbrush and then how to cut a slit and anchor the razor blade onto the end.

Race relations are rock bottom. Blacks sit here, whites there, Hispanics there; all nationalities stick together in groups and there is little intermingling or friendliness between the races. The blacks are angry that Razzberry has a white cellmate, but the black dude who runs a store out of his cell backs Razzberry up and tells the others not to screw with him or Hobart.

In the back of the day room, on tables, like a little flea market, are items prisoners sell like magazines, cigarettes, snacks, coffee grounds, and drugs. You can buy any drug you want; the turnkeys don't care. Standing behind the sellers is a row of what they call punks, male prostitutes wearing do-rags and acting flirty. Razzberry and Hobart sit in there watching *American Bandstand* on one of the TVs. A black dude comes up behind a Hispanic guy watching sports on another TV and slits his throat. Total chaos. Everybody's scrambling and yelling. Blacks and Hispanics brawl. Razzberry and Hobart go to the back of the room to get as far away as possible as the Goon Squad marches in with shields and billy clubs. They fire cannisters of stingers, balls that explode in the air with electric charges. Razzberry and Hobart crawl to the door and are grabbed by the Goon Squad and pulled out into the corridor. The Hispanic man bleeds out while the squad focuses on controlling the inmates.

One day Razzberry is in his cell on the top bunk listening to music. Hobart, on the bottom bunk, reads a magazine. A big black dude, this guy who is always whistling at Razzberry, comes up to the cell and puts his hands on the bars. He says to Razzberry, "When this door opens, I'm gonna come in there and I'm gonna have my way with you." He looks at Hobart and tells him, "You best beat feet, bitch."

"Oh, okay," Razzberry says, brandishing his shank. "No problem. When that door opens, you come on in here. Either I'm gonna die or you're gonna die." He jumps down off the top bunk and stands at the back of the cell holding the shank. Hobart gets up and stands beside him with his. The dude outside the cell stares them down as the minutes go by. Razzberry and Hobart don't move, they don't say anything, and they don't stop staring back at him. When the buzzer goes off, the latches click and the cell door opens. The would-be rapist tells them off and turns and goes about his business.

After seven weeks working the fields, Razzberry puts in for a job in the welding squad. He learned welding at Boys Ranch in agricultural classes and welded bars and gates at the hog farm. He gets the job and leaves the torture of the fields for the indoors, where the welding boss brings them cold soda pop in a cooler. He works with two other guys, but when they leave, he becomes the head welder and does it the rest of his time.

Working helps pass the time and lets him get away from the larger prison population for the bulk of the day. The hatred and violence, the prejudice by all the races toward all the other races, the ever-present danger of being set upon by the crazed, by the sexual predators, and by the sudden, random berserkers, all this has a way of hardening Razzberry as the months pass. Another time, he sees a man get stabbed in the back of the neck, but he and Hobart run back to their cell before everything is locked down. Another time, in the dayroom again and watching TV, an argument breaks out over a punk. The pimp demands his money but the guy won't pay up, saying no. The pimp stabs the man in the stomach. Razzberry and Hobart are caught up in the melee, pulverized by the stingers the Goon Squad fires at them, and roughed up as they scramble to get to safety.

At 3 a.m., near the end of his sentence, Razzberry hears the turnkeys yelling for him. He gets out of bed and puts on pants and boots and shirt. They ship him off to Huntsville and their red walls, home of Texas's capital punishment, once the electric chair and now the lethal injection chamber. Most prisoners go there prior to release. He watches TV for three days, and then they give him a check for two hundred dollars and tell him he better not be in town when the sun sets.

He says he's got more stories that he'll tell me later. Says he hasn't even gotten to the good stuff, and by good he means worse. I can't imagine what's going to be worse than that. Now, however, he's got to have a beer, and he is making himself ready to venture forth. I tell him he was just dry heaving an hour and a half ago. He should take it easy.

"That wouldn't be Razz."

I hand him his bright-orange bucket hat. "Put this on so I can find you if we get separated."

After applying deodorant to his armpits, he changes into a different shirt, saying it matches the orange hat better. It doesn't.

It's a yellow Tweety Bird T-shirt. I give him a look of sad disapproval, which he sees and says to me, "Tweety Bird is cool as shit."

"Get your cane and come on. Oh, but look, I have a present for you." I hand him the joint Heidi gave me.

"My true brother!" He does a little dance.

I lead him through the maze of densely packed tents. He trips over tent lines and falls twice. When we get to the entrance to Centeroo, where people are searched before going through to the stages, the security guy tells Razz he can't bring in his cane. When asked why, he says it's the policy. It could be used as a weapon, so it's not allowed inside. He takes it and sets it off to the side in a large pile of confiscated items, mainly umbrellas and chairs that aren't sufficiently low-rise for these power-mad security people. I'm outraged and tell him no, that's impossible. I want to speak with a supervisor. He yells out, "Diane!"

Diane says there are no exceptions and that we can pick it up when we go back to camp.

I borrow a line from Bea Arthur: "God will get you for that." I used to love it when she said that on the TV show *Maude*. I loved Maude, but my mother wouldn't let us watch her because Maude was such a liberal and an atheist. I wish my mother was here now and could see all this shit. Maybe I shouldn't have taken a hit off Razzberry's joint. Too many dumb thoughts. All he and I do is laugh and giggle.

We go on without his cane. He has to throw his left leg forward and limp along. I tell him when we find a tree, I'm going to get a big branch for him to use as a cane. He says no, no, we have to find beer first. Thirty yards down the dirt road, as hundreds of people pass us in either direction, we stop and huddle together laughing, unable to get it under control. We don't even know why we're laughing.

We pass by the Drive By Truckers playing on a stage too crowded to get anywhere near, and head toward the main Bonnaroo stage. The crowd is thick. Arm in arm we go, slowly, methodically making it step by step through the ten thousand people in front of us. He wants me to get him as close to the front as we can because the Allman Brothers Band is about to take the stage. Those poems of his I read made me so sad, I'm determined more than ever to show him the good side of life. He holds onto me and I hold onto him to keep him from falling, to keep him upright through the crowd. It takes a long while, but we eventually get down as close to the stage as we're going to get, too dense for me to get him any further. We're not only by the stage, but close to the big jumbotron TV that will focus on the band when they start. Now I attempt the impossible and leave him there in the orange hat, snake my way through to the side of the field, and get us beers for the show. How do I make it back with two giant cups of beer, inching my way through people who aren't that happy with me? I do. A lot of beer has to be consumed along the way and a fair amount sloshes out, but Razzberry doesn't mind. He hails me as the hero I am when I see him just as the band starts.

They play "Midnight Rider," then "The Night They Drove Old Dixie Down," and then "Melissa." Razzberry fires up the joint we have left over. When they play "The Whipping Post," Razzberry is in tears, and I know it's what he feels, that he's tied to the whipping post of life. I put my arm over his shoulder and try not to cry.

For all of the long walk back to camp, either my arm is over his shoulder or his arm is over mine, because without the cane, he wears himself out trying to walk and then can't go anymore. I'll find a tree and get a branch for a cane tomorrow. We'll stash it inside

Centeroo past the gestapo, and it'll be there for us in the days ahead. That's the plan. We don't bother looking for his cane in the pile of confiscated crap because it's dark and it would take forever. When we get back, I get him some fajitas from Shakedown Street and a couple of beers and waters to tide him over. I get the rainflys over the tents and put our sleeping bags and pillows in them and make sure he is comfortable. He promises not to go anywhere and that if he needs to pee, he'll pee beside the truck and not try to go to any port-a-potties. I'll just be gone an hour or so, going to check out the Dave Matthews Band, who I've never seen.

Will it be the boring, unoriginal, over-rated, pseudo-sensitive, irritating crap music I heard it was? Will the crowd be obnoxious frat boys and arrogant sorority sluts and yuppies who rollerblade and drink Merlot? I hope not. When I get there and mix in the crowd and listen to Dave Matthews, I'm not impressed. I feel curmudgeonly, but when they play a cover of "Time of the Season" by the Zombies, a sense of the sixties is in the air. The crowd sings the words, people dance, they pass around joints, topless women hula hoop, people on ecstasy make out and dry hump, and I end up having a good time.

I trudge back to camp and make sure Razzberry is okay. He's in his chair up in the bed of the truck, drinking a beer, smoking a joint, and watching the fireworks. It makes me happy.

Chapter Fourteen

In the morning, I slog through mud to Shakedown Street, where I buy two orders of French toast and a large coffee with a double shot of Baileys. While I wait, I look down at my dirty feet and see a plastic baggy with something in it. Pot. There's no one around to claim it; most everyone partied into the wee hours and is still crashed out in their tents. On the way back to camp, a mud pit sucks in one of my flip flops. I wobble on one foot and use my toes to try and pry the flip flop loose. Hot coffee sloshes on my hand. A bee dive bombs my French toast. I overreact, and syrup pours off the paper plate onto my arm and down the side of my shorts. I wobble worse and have to plant my bare foot in the mud. Somehow, I still make it back to the campsite with some food and coffee intact.

Razzberry and I share the coffee and eat the French toast while we look over the music schedule. He doesn't want to do too much walking, especially without his cane, because of how painful and exhausting it is for him. He also doesn't want to take his pills, blaming them for what happened yesterday. Pot would make it more bearable, he says, smiling. I produce the ground score baggie I found and hand it to him. After his exaggerated disbelief and the comments he makes about how I'm not as square as people think, we come up with a plan to anchor Razzberry at a particular spot at the main Bonnaroo stage where he can stay put all day. No walking back and forth to camp. I'll bring him food and keep him supplied with beer, so he can just sit and enjoy the music.

"Who's playing on the main stage?"

I look at the schedule and tell him, "Government Mule, the Black Crowes, and Widespread Panic."

"That'll work."

We hear a voice calling out through the campgrounds, "Bloody Marys, get your Bloody Marys." Oh hell yes. The guy sits with us while he fixes two drinks and even has olives to put in them. We don't have to get going for a couple of hours. We can relax. Razzberry rolls up a joint. I want to hear more of his stories and what happened to him after he gets out of the state pen. Here is what he tells me.

When they let him out of Huntsville, he cashes his two-hundred-dollar prison check, goes straight to a store to get tennis shoes and a warmup suit to wear, and rides the bus back to Amarillo. An ex–Boys Rancher who was in Anderson Dorm picks him up and lets him stay with him and his wife on the couch. He goes about catching up on all the drinking he didn't get to do for the last two years and gets a job installing sprinkler systems.

When he gets off parole, the hard-core partying begins. At a bar, he meets Timmy, a big white guy from Arkansas, and they hit it off smoking pot and getting drunk. They get an apartment together in Amarillo. Razzberry finds a job making better money with Harmon Steel Erection Company so he can pay his half of the rent and the bills.

The landlady, after they lived there for two weeks, sees him walking up the sidewalk to the apartment and asks him, "Why do I keep seeing you around here?"

"I live here."

"No, you don't. I would know."

"I'm in 131 with Timmy."

"Oh, hell no. I don't allow your kind to live here," she yells, except she uses the N-word instead of "your kind." She confronts Timmy and says he didn't tell her a black man was living there, except she uses the N-word again. They have to move. Be out by the end of the week, they're told.

Razzberry goes and opens the phone book and calls a lawyer. The first lawyer he speaks with says he'll take care of it at no charge. After the landlady gets a call and is told what's what, she backs down. She gets all riled up when Razzberry parades his white girlfriend up and down the sidewalk in front of the office and says as he passes by, "I wish a nice day for you, ma'am."

Timmy isn't the best role model for Razzberry, especially when it comes to intravenous drugs, shooting up speed, and dealing drugs. He sells pot, cocaine, speed, any and everything except heroin. Razzberry takes his advice to get a gun. Timmy drives Razzberry to the Tip Top Club to buy a gun but sends him in alone since it's an all-black club and he's not allowed in there. Razzberry drinks two beers with the seller, gives him fifty dollars, and is handed a brown paper sack with a pearl-handled magnum. People come to their apartment to buy drugs. Razzberry's job is to sit on the couch and just observe, his gun beside him, because there's always the chance of somebody coming in there and trying to rob them. Timmy also brings him along when he goes to collect money. One customer owes eight hundred dollars. When they go inside, they pull their guns and have five men with guns cocked, pointing at them, but they get their money.

One day they get some speed from a guy who tells them no matter what, only shoot up 10 cc because it's strong as hell. Is it that good? Yeah, the guys says, no matter what, only 10 cc. When they get home to the apartment, Rhonda, a woman always buying cocaine and speed from them, waits beside their door. They go in and sell her hers. She goes in the bathroom to shoot up; they shoot up on the couch. They forget to tell her about the 10 cc maximum. They're on the couch feeling the rush when they hear Rhonda's head hit the bathroom floor. Timmy jumps on her and thumps her in the chest. He does it again and again.

Razzberry says, "I think she's dead."

Timmy stands and looks down at Rhonda and says, "Maybe she is."

"Yeah, she's dead, man," Razzberry says.

"She looks dead."

"That bitch is dead."

"Let's take her out to the alley by the dumpster."

"Good idea."

"She can't stay in the bathroom."

"Nope."

They carry her by her hands and feet out the back door, through the gate into the alley and lay her down behind the dumpster. They go back inside, sit on the couch, drink whiskey, and smoke a joint while watching *Miami Vice*. Crockett and Tubbs find out the undercover FBI agent they're working with is a total asshole.

Timmy tells Razzberry he has to see the movie *Red Dawn*, about the Soviet Union invading America and these people who fight back.

"Who's in it?" Razzberry asks.

"I don't know. Why does it matter who's is in it? It's about fighting the damn communists, man."

"I'm all for that."

Their back door swings open and slams against the wall. Rhonda stands there, seething. Her hair makes her look like she's been electrocuted, sticking up with leaves and twigs in it.

"You sons of bitches!"

"Oh, hey, Rhonda," Timmy says, giving her a wave.

She stomps past them and goes into the bathroom. "Where's my shit?"

"Here," Timmy says, "on the coffee table."

She snatches her plastic baggy off the table, and says, "You sons of bitches," as she goes to the door. "Gonna leave me to die."

Timmy tells her, "You knew what you were getting into." She glares at him before slamming the door behind her. They bust out laughing and go back to the whiskey and *Miami Vice*.

Not long after, Razzberry gets a woman pregnant and moves out of Timmy's, and in with her. He gets a job at the beef plant on the killing floor, and then takes various other jobs there defacing, dehorning, and ripping tails. His marriage doesn't last long but it's a doozy and they break up and get back together several times over a short period. Through the early and middle nineties, he takes his son and his son's friends fishing and camping at Boys Ranch, on the other side of the ranch at Magenta where I got bit by the scorpion and where turtles ate the catfish on my stringer. They swim in the ponds and paddle around on rafts, cook fish over the campfire, and explore the old ghost town of Cheyenne that washed away in a flood in the 1890s.

Speed, though, is his problem. Too much speed. Shooting it up. His little boy walking in and seeing him do it. Disappearing. Forgetting where he is supposed to be. Not showing up when he is scheduled to pick up his son. Getting in fights in bars. Going from speed being the problem, to cocaine. The beef plant lets him go, and he starts back working for a landscaping company. One day, Mr. and Mrs. Ohls, two of his customers that were also Boys Ranch donors from way back, listen to him talk about wanting to start his own landscaping and flower bed business called Razz's Yard Rejuvenation. His company would provide year-round care and maintenance for a thirty-five-dollar fee as well as custom-built flower beds out of landscaping timbers and stones. He would build them, plant them, care for them, and install a drip system if that's what the customers want. Mr. Ohls says he will back him and offers to buy all the lawn equipment and other tools and supplies Razzberry needs to get going, including a truck.

Everything goes well at the beginning. Pieces of paper advertising Razz's Yard Rejuvenation can be seen on Toot-n-Totem convenience store bulletin boards all over town. He shamelessly steals customers from his previous employers, especially Boys Ranch retirees and bigwigs. It's not long, though, until cocaine and speed derail his train. The expense of his habit overwhelms him. He sells the truck and the equipment and goes out of business in no time. Crying on the phone, he tells Mrs. Ohls that he's sorry for wasting their money and ruining their faith in him. He tells her about the drug issues and that he's been homeless for the last two weeks. She gives him her love and tells him she'll talk to Mr. Ohls and see if they can help him. He's supposed to call back in a few days.

He calls back and speaks to Mr. Ohls, who tells him he's going to help him with his addictions. Tomorrow, if he goes to the Northwest Texas Hospital in Amarillo, Mr. Ohls will meet him there and pay for the medicine to ease withdrawals and stop cravings. He goes there and meets Mr. Ohls and two doctors. They tell him they want to give him a shot to make the cravings go away. One of the doctors brings over the needle. He rolls up his sleeve.

When he wakes up, he feels groggy. He is in a bed and he's wearing a hospital gown. He gets up disoriented and dizzy, grabs ahold of the wall, and moves toward the door. Hugging the walls, he goes down the corridor into a big day room with people spread out on couches and sitting at tables. At the front of the room is a caged-off area with nurses behind it handing out medicine to a line of patients. He goes to the front and asks the nurse, "Where am I?"

"Settle down," she replies. "It'll be okay."

"No cutting in line," a female patient says. "Why are you letting him cut in line?" She starts shouting. "Why are you letting him cut in line? How is that fair? How is that fair?"

The nurse tells him, "Go to the back of the line!"

"Where am I?"

"Go to the back of the line and I'll talk to you when it's your turn."

"Why is he allowed to cut in line?" the woman screams. "This is what's wrong!"

"Becky, please!" the nurse says to her and shoots her a nasty look.

Razzberry stumbles away and sits at a nearby table. A woman looking like a stand-in for Nora Desmond in *Sunset Boulevard* sits across from him with a little mirror and a makeup kit. She glances at him as she puts on lipstick. "Am I pretty?" she asks.

He doesn't want to tell her that her makeup is over-the-top hideous. "Yeah, sure," he says.

"No, really. Am I pretty?" She's suddenly emotional and near tears.

"Yeah, you're kind of pretty."

Her lower lip quivers. "Kind of?"

"You're very pretty, okay? God!" He gets up and goes to the window to see if he can find out where he is. A man with his arms out to his sides makes airplane noises and flies around the room. Most of the people sit stupefied like zombies. Nora Desmond comes up like she's never seen him before, smiling and flirtatious, asking, "Am I pretty?" He tries ignoring her and looks out the window. She doesn't stop asking. "Do you think I'm pretty? Am I pretty? Do I have a pretty face?"

"Yeah, you're very pretty. Don't ask me no more." He knows he's flown over the cuckoo's nest.

Her bottom lip starts quivering. He goes and gets in line to talk to the nurse behind the cage. The nurse says he's here on doctor's orders. He takes the cup of water she slides to him and the cup of pills.

"I need to see you take them and swallow them."

He puts the pills in his mouth and washes them down.

The pills act quickly. Disoriented and groggy, he sinks down onto a couch before he can get back to his room. He sits there an hour or more, not thinking any thoughts, not even aware of anything really, until an orderly tells him he's peed himself and escorts him out to change into a new gown.

Four days of being tranquilized pass by, but finally he plots an escape. When they give him the cup of pills, he pretends to swallow them and once he gets away from the cage, he pulls them out from under his tongue. He uses a telephone in an unoccupied office and asks the girlfriend he's been knocking boots with to come get him. He stays with her a couple of weeks until the girlfriend's other boyfriend who she said would never get out of prison, gets out of prison and throws all Razzberry's clothes and things into the mud.

Homeless again, he lives on the streets in Amarillo for weeks until he moves to the city dump and into a huge concrete-drainage culvert. Nobody bothers him there. When it gets cold, he stays at the Faith City Mission, but they kick everyone out during the day, sending him roaming around town and hoping to get a handout from somebody.

"That was when I had life, man," he says, hanging his head. "I squandered it."

"You still have life," I tell him. "This is life. Come on and let's go, we're not going to squander Bonnaroo."

He gets his cane and dons the orange hat. "I'm just worthless, man."

"You need to forgive yourself. Jesus forgave you, why can't you?"

Rain clouds darken and approach from the south. We take ponchos and head out, his arm over my shoulder or his hand holding onto my arm. I'm going to find him a big stick for a cane when we get through security, I promise him. We go slowly down the road joined at the hip, people passing by staring and looking surprised when their eyes light on us. Maybe it's the salt and pepper they see that's making them smile.

I ask Razzberry if I should tell them about the insane asylum and he tells me to shut my face. The line through security is long but when we emerge on the side, Razzberry tells me to hold on and stops to fish out his lighter. He produces the joint he smuggled through security and fires it up. He says he's got the whole bag in his pocket. We toke up in front of God and everybody.

Further on, I see a shirtless guy sitting up in a tree he's not supposed to climb. I call out to him, "Hey, dude! See my buddy?" I point to Razzberry. "They confiscated his cane. Can you break off a branch that might work as a cane for him?"

The guy looks down at me and doesn't say anything; he just sits there. I get closer and call out louder to him, thinking he must not be able to hear me. Still the guy remains speechless and motionless. I tell Razzberry, "Forget it. He's up in the cuckoo's nest, this guy. He tripping."

"Throw something at him," Razzberry urges. I look around for something to throw but don't see anything. We keep trucking.

The main stage has twenty thousand people packed in front of it. We get beers and slice our way through the crowd to the spot he selects to be his home base. We watch Government Mule as the rain clouds press toward us. A free-spirited young woman next to us smiles and starts talking to us, telling us her name is Margarita Malarkey. I find that impossible to believe. She shows me her driver's license. Three minutes later, she and her boyfriend make out so passionately on the ground that we are forced to relocate.

Just after I leave Razzberry to go over to another stage and see Jack Johnson, the rain hits. It's torrential. Fat, cold raindrops pour down. Thunder and lightning. I slip my poncho on and go to a nearby stage under a large tent that fits three or four hundred people. When I get there, it's packed inside and I find a spot just barely out of the rain, right on the edge. Behind me, hundreds of people stand in ankle-deep mud unable to get out of the rain, but so desperate to see the band that they continue standing there. I spot several women tied for first place in the wet T-shirt situation going on behind me.

As soon as the rain lets up a little, I hurry back to the main stage to check on Razzberry and bring him a beer. The orange hat trick is genius. Without it, I'd never find him in the crowd. He's in high spirits right where I left him in the open, dancing and dancing in his poncho to the Black Crowes. I stand back and watch him for a while, happy for him. We party hard, drink many beers, and toke many tokes. After Widespread Panic, he's wiped out, and it's difficult and slow going the whole way back to camp.

I end the night by leaving him while he sleeps in his tent and go down at midnight to watch Trey Anastasio perform. I buy a couple of shots of tequila and a strong vodka drink along the way. I pass out in the crowd, face first in the mud. When I regain consciousness, two college boys are carrying me through the crowd to a medical golf cart that pulls up. They put me on the back and we take off to the medical tent, speeding over rough terrain. Big bumps almost throw me off, so I have to hang on with both hands. At the medical tent, they usher me toward the staff, but I stop and take a bottle of water off a table and tell them, no, I'm going home. You need to get checked out, they insist. I say, look, if I survived Mr. Toad's wild ride that I just went on, I think I'm okay to make it back.

On the final day, Razzberry and I see Matisyahu, a Hasidic Jew singing a mixture of reggae and rap, and we see My Morning Jacket, a band that has people wearing nine-foot-tall puppets dancing onstage with them; a giraffe, a cow, George Washington, and a big bug with green orbs for eyes. We end Bonnaroo by seeing my favorite band, one I've seen dozens of times all over the Southeast: Donna the Buffalo. The first time I saw them, I was hooked. They don't fit into any category of music I know, but sometimes it's

Americana, sometimes Zydeco, sometimes jam band, always uplifting and always good for the soul. They are the one band I really need Razzberry to see before he goes back to Amarillo. For all I know, we may never have a chance to go to music festivals together again if his spinal condition worsens like he says it will. He may end up not being able to walk. His scheduled surgery is to remove the two big lumps on his back, not to resolve the underlying problem. There is no resolution for that; it's degenerative.

We hobble our way to the stage early and score a spot up close. Soon we're pinned in by the crowd behind us. With smiles on our faces, we watch the show and dance side by side with everybody else swaying and gyrating all around us.

When the show is over, two beautiful college girls who had been standing right behind us during the show, ask us if they can take our picture and ask if we will be in a picture with them. They tell us, "You two made our whole Bonnaroo."

We pose for pictures and head back to camp talking about how two geezers from Boys Ranch made those college girls' festival. We must be doing something right.

Chapter Fifteen

The passing tropical storm flattens tents and canopies all through the campground. Ours survives. Razzberry is wiped out and wants to crash. I relocate his tent away from the tailpipe so I don't gas him with carbon monoxide. Since they're broadcasting the main stage on a radio station, I sit in the truck and listen to Widespread Panic while he snoozes. Under the dome light, I look through Razzberry's poems and journal entries in the old spiral notebooks and papers in his bookbag. Everything is handwritten and becomes less and less legible over time. All of them are dated and some have notes at the top or bottom that provide context. Written at Kelly and Dee's. Written at the Potter County Jail. Jobless and lonely. At the Resource Center. Headed to the streets and homeless. Written for my son. Losing control of my body. Formby State Prison in isolation. Dozens and dozens of the poems are all written for the same woman, all with similar themes. How could you hurt me so bad? Why won't you come find me? God, can you give her back to me? Her name appears a thousand times: Jeannie. Her eyes, he writes from jail, are as blue as the panhandle. He wants to grow old with her and sit in rocking chairs.

She never came back to see if I was hungry or cold
How could you turn your back on me?
She never came back to see if I needed her love
How could you throw me away?
She didn't see me breaking down, crying in the dark
Left me in a ditch
A dog in the rain
Never tried to find me
Nobody wants a broken down man
Nobody ever will
So I got blown up yesterday
Did you see me lose the war?
I wish you could see me now with my bad limp
The only one I'll ever love went away
She didn't want to dodge the mine field with me

Nobody died here and cried here but me
Nobody lost their heart and soul here or even cared here
but me
Nobody gave their all here and lost it all here but me
Nobody got left here and is alone here but me
And nobody has feelings here or has any hope here
Not even me

Hey Razz, you're never going to be a good father. You're
as low as they get
Hey Razz, the world has given up on the fisherman
Hey Razz, your mom and dad are ashamed
Hey Razz, you're never going to live in the country

Hey Razz, do you think Ken Arthur and you will ever
meet again
Hey Razz, Boys Ranch will bring you to the country when
you die at least

On the long ride back to my house in south Georgia, after we
pig out at a Waffle House just down the interstate from Bonnaroo,
I get him to tell me about Jeannie. He says he's still not over her
and then goes into it.

He meets her when he takes too many drugs and people at the Faith
City Mission take him to the hospital to get his stomach pumped.
Jeannie's a nurse. He cracks jokes and makes her laugh. When he
gets out, she comes looking for him at the shelter and voila, they get
an apartment together. She saves him from the streets. He gets a job
with a horticulture company for a while and then gets a better job
as a diesel mechanic, where he learns to change out the rear ends of
eighteen-wheelers. Pulling transmissions isn't easy; they're heavy,
and when you are beneath the engines, you just have to manhandle
them. He's small, and the other mechanics are surprised he can do it.

Razzberry and Jeannie have a drug-fueled relationship. They do
cocaine every chance they get, and before long it takes its inevitable
toll. He gets fired from the mechanic's shop for being late all the
time, being strung out on drugs, and getting surly with the boss.
He'd worked there a while and has fifteen hundred dollars in a
savings plan. He cashes that out and spends the money on drugs. He
goes back to work for a landscaping company. Everybody working
landscaping is on drugs, so he knows he'll fit in a lot better there.

Jeannie has a daughter who Razzberry has helped raise since she was ten years old. Now she's fifteen and has a boyfriend that Razzberry doesn't like. One weekend, Razzberry's twelve-year-old son and his little friend stay with them but Razzberry has to go to Oklahoma overnight to buy drugs. When he comes home the next day, his son tells him that he went on a wild ride with Jenny's boyfriend. He tells Razzberry that they sped up and down Amarillo Boulevard, screaming at people, racing through neighborhoods, swerving, and doing donuts on city streets until after midnight.

When the boyfriend comes over, Razzberry confronts him about it. The boyfriend walks to him sitting on the couch, looms over him, does a flex, and makes a loud aggressive growl in his face. From the couch, Razzberry punches him in the mouth. The dude falls backward. Razzberry is on him in a flash and punches him in the face over and over. One of Razzberry's buddies sitting there tells him to take it easy. Razzberry stands the guy up and lands a haymaker on his jaw that sends him crashing through the sheetrock, exposing the lumber. Now Razzberry gets a knife from the kitchen, but his buddy stops him by grabbing the kid by the shirt and by the blue jeans and flinging him through the air into the driveway.

Jeannie kicks him out of the house for that, but then they get back together. They split up several times, and finally Razzberry has to get his own apartment elsewhere. He gets a job working for Mrs. Ladd, a rich woman who gives him $350 a week to work at her big house. He does landscaping and yardwork for her, and takes care of her golden retrievers. She has massive portraits in the foyer and on the mantle of her walking golden retrievers at dog shows.

He makes up with Jeannie, and they go back to doing drugs together. One day when he gets paid and gets a bonus from the rich lady, he goes out and buys a big pink rock of speed—grade-A stuff—some cocaine, and an assortment of other drugs. A fishing buddy comes over to his apartment and they snort a couple of lines of coke. The take the mirror they're using to snort the line and put the meth rock and a little pile of cocaine on it and then put it in the bathroom beside the sink. Jeannie comes over and brings along a friend named Dewayne. Razzberry tells them the stuff is in the bathroom and to help themselves and he goes out on the balcony to smoke a cigarette with his fishing buddy.

A squad car turns into the apartments and pulls up below. They figure the law is here because of the downstairs neighbors who are always fighting and getting the cops called on them, but then they hear the two officers coming up the stairs and banging on the door. Razzberry opens it and asks if he can help them. They say they got a call that he was dealing drugs out of the apartment. Razzberry says no, he's not selling anything. They ask to come in and look around. Thinking Jeannie and DeWayne must have heard the knocking and the cops and hidden the stuff in the bathroom, Razzberry says, "Come on in."

Jeannie and Dewayne round the corner toward the officers, clueless, snowblind, and with white powder around their nostrils. The cops sit them all down and one of them goes into the bathroom and brings back the mirror covered with drugs. They all go to jail. Razzberry, not wanting Jeannie to get in trouble with her nursing job, takes the rap and admits all the drugs are his. The others are bailed out, but Razzberry's bail is once again set too high and he's stuck in jail. The first night he has to sleep on the floor beside the commode because the jail is full, but he doesn't go to sleep at all because of the speed in his system.

Dear Jeannie,

Well, I'm not going to try to sound down and out but that Joe guy never came through so I'm not getting bailed out. I guess I'll be here until I go to court because I can't get anybody to bail me out. That's sad. I've helped so many people and we can't get one of our so-called friends to help me. I don't understand the world today but I'm trying not to hate. Please don't leave me all alone but I would understand if you did. You're the only one that believes in me now. I hope everything is okay on the home front. Have you been watering the flowers? Did you remember to fertilize them every now and then? Did you get the fertilizer from Perry? Get the blue stuff. How is the car running? Have you checked the oil and the coolant? There's some in the trunk if you need it. Have you heard from my son? I hope he doesn't hate me. I love him, but I'm not worth a damn as a father, am I. Tell him I love him and I'm sorry for everything. I think the Lord is making me sit here for a reason. I guess that why he didn't have that Joe guy bail me out. I hope He has a plan for us. Don't let your Razz go. But I have thought that if I got out I'd get my backpack and just split because the way I see it, I don't have a friend except you. I wish I could just wander all over with my backpack and my headphones going from town to town and seeing the countryside. But running would take me farther from my son and I would never leave you. I hope you've slowed down on that stuff. It's brought us nothing but down. Maybe one day when I'm out and we're doing good again, but I don't know if we even need to play. Can you call Mrs. Ladd and see if she will bail me out? I will pay her back. Love, your country boy, Razz.

After a week in jail, the rich lady with the golden retrievers goes to the bail bondsman and pays it. She's never accusatory or judgmental toward him and doesn't require him to pay it back, only to get cleaned up and straighten out his life.

His court-appointed lady lawyer isn't going to be able to do much for him, he thinks, and with the rest of his criminal record, he figures he's going to get put away for a long time. He gets back with Jeannie in the meantime, but running from the law is on his mind. Taking his backpack and hitchhiking someplace far away has a lot of appeal. The lawyer tells him that the prosecutor wants him to do twenty-five years in prison, but she fought that and whittled it down to ten years. She keeps fighting for him until she gets a deal that if he pleads guilty, he'll only have to serve fifteen months, but he will have to do every day of it because there will be no option for "good time" early release.

It snows for two days straight, but the morning he goes to court to face the music and prison again, there is a perfect blue sky. He gets up early and makes coffee while Jeannie sleeps. He thinks about his son and how he isn't going to get to see him for a long time. His son wasn't happy with him over the weekend and hardly spoke a word. How will he ever make up for being so bad of a father so many times, giving his boy all that pain that he's holding inside? All those times taking him and his friends out to Boys Ranch to camp and fish doesn't mean anything compared to all the negative. All the times he wasn't there for him. He cries looking at a picture of his boy when he was little.

He watches Jeannie sleep, hating that they're being torn apart because of drugs. They've been barely surviving because of the money problems. They've have out so many hot checks. The rent is past due, and so is her car payment. Everything is falling apart. He cooks her breakfast and brushes her hair and tells her how much he hates leaving her to face all the problems.

They're silent on the long drive to the courthouse. When he gets out, they have one final embrace and he hands her the note he wrote the night before.

> Well, Jeannie, the time has come. It's here. We can't go on this way no more. We have to make our lives right. We've hurt our kids, screwed up everything. We have to get back to real life. The drugs have killed us. Look down at our arms, then you'll know what I'm talking about. You've got to get back on track while I'm away. Make life better for yourself. You have to be strong and get back to the real Jeannie. I want you to be that nurse again. I love you and hate to have to go away but I'll be back, that's a promise. My heart hurts having to go away for so long. Don't let your Razz go. I'm coming back. You're the only woman I want to grow old with. Promise to wait for me until I get back.

With no possibility of getting out early, Razzberry doesn't bother respecting the guards or doing what he is told when he gets to Formby State Jail outside of Plainview, Texas. Most of his time is spent segregated from others and in isolation. The prison usually puts drug offenders together in a ward where they take classes about drugs and how to rehabilitate themselves. He hates the old lady that runs it. He cusses her out, so he's put back in isolation. They take him out of his cell in handcuffs. Anywhere he goes, he's in handcuffs. He fills several spiral notebooks with poems about Jeannie and about his dream of getting out of Amarillo and off the drugs and living in the country.

"Razzberry's Faraway Place"
Birds singing in the morning
Coffee being made
Long summer days spent fishing
Riding the horses
Making snow angels
Skating on frozen ponds
Slopping the hogs
Smelling the country air
Rooster crowing in the morning
A shack and a potbellied stove
A dog following me into the woods

"Questions"
Can you meet me when this is over with?
Will you still love me when it's all said and done?
Can the puzzle pieces still fit together?
Do you still want to hold me?
Do you believe in me?
Will you throw me away?

Oh God, do you remember me?

I'm the one that keeps asking about living in the country

I know you're tired of hearing me

I know I haven't walked in your steps

But I've been caged for so long

Do you know how it feels to be caged?

Every day the same thing.

So God, do you think you could help ol Razz?

I just want to be the ol country boy I am.

Signed Your Country Boy Razz

Jeannie picks him up when he is released from prison. He's had no happier day in a long time. He's got it in his mind to finally do right and get back on track. On the way to her house, Jeannie stops and buys crack, speed, cocaine, and a bag full of pot for him, all with her money because he has none. All his resistance evaporates in a flash. He goes back to shooting up drugs. Their rekindled relationship goes south in short order and they're on again and off again, arguing, throwing things at the walls, and she finally leaves him for good. He's homeless, living on the streets of Amarillo, eating at the Salvation Army and the Faith City Mission. A fishing buddy lets him sleep on his back porch, but when he goes to work, he locks up the house and Razzberry has to stay outside and drink water from a hose.

Two months after Jeannie leaves him, he has the stroke that shuts down the left side of his body and lands him in the hospital. All the next year, he writes poems wishing Jeannie would come find him and give him another chance, poems to God to give her back to him, the poems to himself about how hopeless and broken he is and how he will never win.

We're south of Macon when he finishes the story. He looks out the window on the verge of tears and tells me that he wishes he didn't have to tell me so many shameful things about himself, that he sure would like to give a better account of himself to Boys Ranch. I tell him to stifle it. We lived life, I tell him. Now we need to learn from it, that's all. I put in a Donna the Buffalo CD and let the music administer healing. We roll down the interstate and it's not long until I can tell from the smile on his face and how he's dancing in his seat that the music is working.

Chapter Sixteen

The park is full of Sunday fathers and melted ice cream
We try to do the best within the given time
A kid should be with his mother
Everybody knows that
What can a father do but babysit sometimes?
— Sting, "I'm So Happy That I Can't Stop Crying"

The kids get to come see me this weekend. Their mother, the soon to be ex-wife, drops them off out front. When they come into the living room with their bags, I introduce them to Razzberry. Kacey, my boy, is seventeen and hilarious. Chelsea, fifteen, she's shy, overcoming autism and is an incredible artist and *Pokémon* savant among other talents. When she starts talking *Pokémon*, Razzberry squints and cocks his head like a confused German Shepherd. We take him into Chelsea's room to a poster on the wall with dozens of *Pokémon* characters. I cover up one of their names and ask Chelsea, "Which one is this one?"

"Charmander," she replies.

"Okay, and what are Charmander's powers?"

"Blaze and Solar Power."

"How tall is Charmander?"

"Two feet tall."

I cover a different character's name and ask her which one it is. "Jigglypuff."

"What are his powers?"

"Cute Charm and Friend Guard."

Razzberry is impressed. Kacey tells him that he should see her drawings. She pulls a sketchbook out of her backpack and shows Razzberry her drawings of dragons. He says wow as he looks at each one, and remarks on how intricate they are with the details of the scales, the horns, the way they look three dimensional.

"Kacey, here," I tell Razzberry, "is my number one son."

Kacey smiles and points a finger at himself, nodding. I put my arm over Kacey's shoulder and ask him, "What should I tell Razzberry about you?"

"That I'm awesome."

"Okay, there's that, but what else? Okay, Kacey has terrible taste in music."

"No, I don't. What we swingers were going against were uptight squares like you."

"Oh yeah," I tell Razzberry. "We goof on each other with *Austin Powers* quotes."

We go out to eat at a catfish place where Razzberry tells the kids stories about Boys Ranch and about me and him. Kacey tells embarrassing stories about me like the time I ruined our brand-new microwave by putting a metal pan in there. I tell Razzberry about the time when Kacey was in the fourth grade and had to write a report on a state and design a state coin. The teacher assigned him Arkansas. When I came home from a business trip and went over

his homework, I saw written across the top of the coin the motto
for Arkansas: "Literacy Ain't Everything."

I pointed at it and asked him, "What this?"

"The state motto."

"I don't think so."

"Yes, it is, Dad. I got it off the internet."

Later, when the kids are glued to the TV and Razzberry asks me
about Chelsea, I tell him at first we thought she was deaf, but her
hearing test went fine. Then a doctor diagnosed her with autism and
told us about the spectrum and that she's technically in a category
they call pervasive developmental disorder. No known cause or cure.
It's a neurological disability that affects the ability to communicate,
understand language, and interact with others. We asked what we
could do. The doctor said that, unfortunately, not a lot can be done
and many of these children end up being institutionalized. Turns
out he was a total idiot because he said she'd likely never learn to
use words and we proved him wrong. My father-in-law gave us
twenty-five hundred dollars cash so we could fly in a man from the
Autism Center at UCLA to work with us on a specialized program
for Chelsea. Part of the program involved giving her vitamins such
as B6 and the amino acid Dimethylglycine, DMG. The main part of
the program was known as the Lovaas Method. Dr. Lovaas, from
what we researched, had been successful at reaching autistic children
early on and producing almost miraculous results.

We applied the method. Her mom, Kacey, and I were the
therapists along with some college students who were majoring in
speech communication. In the first month, Chelsea acquired five
hundred words that she could point to when we conducted the trials
where we taught her one word at a time. Fork, spoon, man, woman,

blue, yellow, boy, girl, coat, pants, over, under, up, down, cold, hot, happy, sad, etc. When she started saying the words, it was to us a miraculous breakthrough, like Helen Keller saying the word "water." She even started calling us mom and dad.

The war against autism includes many battles, and one of ours involved our health insurance company. Services recommended by the Center for Autism and Related Disabilities at the University of South Florida were not covered by our insurance. They told us that autism is a disorder, not a disease, and they don't cover disorders. Alcoholism and drug addiction, no problem, they cover whatever you need to get cleaned up, but a child with autism, they get nothing. Not speech therapy, occupational therapy, nada. I had a boss, though, Lou Rivera, who told me to bring all the bills to him and he'd take care of them. And he did. That's true human kindness for you. Great boss.

We fought battles and won major victories. She talks in full sentences, tells jokes, does math and her schoolwork, reads and writes. I show Razzberry some of the first things she wrote that I have in a collection I will keep for the rest of my life. First we look at four special scraps of paper I've kept that she slipped under the bedroom door when she wanted to sleep with us instead of in her room.

Dad! Please would I get in bed with you? Not an ugly troll. Love, Chelsea

She's not a tornado.

No poop in pants.

Will you have fun? ___ Yes or ___ Yes? Love, Chelsea

We go through a pile of her drawings and letters she wrote to me and her mom early on.

Dear Father, I missed you extremely much. I was hoping you had so much fun. Can your car go up to 135 miles per hour? I was hoping we got 6 million dollars. Love, Chelsea

Dear Dad,
  I'm alone and winey
  Tuck me in and kiss me
  Cuddle me and love on me
  You love me, I love you

To: Dad
From: Chelsea
  My Dad is better than the rest of the Dads
  I do everything very very nice to Dad
  My Dad is the best Dad ever
  I love my Dad
  I love your clothes
  I love your voice
  You can do anything your way
  I would love playing games with you
  Every time you leave, I miss you a lot and cannot give
  up missing you

Dear Mom,
  I want to have fun extremely bad
  Give me a charmy behavior, please?
  I'm just an 11 year old heart
  I'm just a young hatless wizard
  Talk light otherwise I'll axidently hurt my feelings
  If I say sorry, I need you to forgive me, or else I'll pretend
  to get sad in front of my Dad.

The next day we get a big box of oysters in the shells and smoke them on the grill. We build a fire and swat gnats. The kids go back to their mom's, and Razzberry and I take off on one final trip before he returns to Amarillo. We head to the Tampa Bay area and Dunedin, Florida, near Clearwater, where we get a hotel close enough to walk to and stumble back from the Dunedin Brewery, a microbrewery and restaurant where Rebekah Pulley is playing. She's the singer that mesmerized Razzberry at Uphonia music festival, and he's in heaven sitting at a table by the stage. I know this because he keeps telling me so. During the break, he goes outside and smokes a cigarette with her. He makes a new friend. When he comes back, he is triumphant.

All we do is laugh and talk about Boys Ranch and the old days. I push him in a wheelchair through the Florida Aquarium, in downtown Tampa. On his final night, back at my house, we build a fire and sit beside it watching the embers and listening to Donna the Buffalo.

"Do you remember when I read to you out of that one book?" I ask.
"No."
"The one about . . . wait, what's the name of it? Oh yeah, 'An

Apparent Intention in the Fate of an Individual.'"

"No."

"When we were talking about the reason things happen and shit like that!"

"Oh, oh yeah."

"I went on and on about what Mr. Price told me, you know, about how things are going to happen and we shouldn't be surprised or thinking it's unfair when it happens, and how there might be a lesson when you look back on things later."

"Oh yeah, now I remember."

"I think you're lying."

"No, I remember."

"Anyway, when I think about this thing that happened to you, that crippled you like this, I wonder what if it didn't happen. Where would you be? What would you be like?"

He thinks about it for quite a while as I stoke the fire.

"That's hard to answer," he says finally.

"Let me ask you this. Do you think you'd be clean and sober, off all the bad drugs?"

After a long hesitation he says, "Probably not."

"Why not?"

"Cause I never really tried to ever step on the brakes. Had no brakes."

"So where do you think you'd be if it hadn't happened? I want to hear your answer."

He thinks for a while and gets up and walks away from the fire into the darkness deeper in the backyard under the pines. When he comes back, he throws a log on the fire and watches the embers go flying. "I probably wouldn't be here with you, brother," he says through sudden tears. "That's the sad part. You want to know the truth? Knowing ol' Razz, I bet I'd be back in prison somehow. All I ever had was bad luck. Or I'd be living on the streets. I'm the king of bad choices, you know that?"

"You might be dead, the way those drugs do you."

"Oh, hell yeah. That's right up there with jail and being homeless. Those are the three things that probably would have happened to me: being homeless, being in prison, or being dead."

"Maybe it's God's way of putting the brakes on you."

"He might've been saving me from something worse."

I nod. "Well, I'm glad I finally found you. Me and Britt Hammond looked for a long time for you."

"I'm so glad we're back together, brother. You showed me real life. I seen the prettiest hippie girls I ever laid eyes on. I feel like a new person. I'm serious, Ken. This has healed me."

"Here, I want to give you this before you get on the bus tomorrow." I reach under my chair and pull out a present I wrapped in Christmas wrapping paper. "I give you this gift to remind you of me, because you're my true brother." I hand it to him.

"You didn't have to get me anything."

"I want this to comfort you on your way back to Amarillo."

"Well, thank you, brother." He rips open the wrapping paper. It's a bag of Starburst with a can of Copenhagen stuffed inside.

"You son of a bitch!" he says. "You ain't never gonna let me forget this, are you?"

"No."

We bust out laughing. I go and get us beers and we sit long into the night.

Chapter Seventeen

Three months after Razzberry rides back on the bus, I am in Pittsburgh at a steel mill when I get a call on my cell phone from a number with the Amarillo area code. I'm wearing a hard hat, safety glasses, and hearing plugs, and standing next to loud machinery with a group of mechanics and production operators. Root Cause Analysis is the class I'm teaching this week. The machine we're looking over is a disaster. In three or four places, somebody used too much grease and it's blowing out bearings. In other places, the grease lines are hardened and stopped up, probably because somebody's been using either the wrong grease or incompatible greases. Oil leaks out over there. The gauges are covered in grime and are unreadable. None of the lubrication points are labeled. The oil filter is in bypass. And they want to know why the machine is so unreliable. As their consultant, I want to be honest and say, look what you're doing to it, you're killing it. I don't, however, because it's better to have them come to that conclusion themselves. I do hope they have an epiphany soon because I really want to slap the shit out of a couple of them.

Meet me in the training room in thirty minutes, I tell the group and go outside to call Razzberry back. He doesn't answer the phone number I redialed. The person who answers is Jeff Price, somebody I haven't seen or spoken with since I was at Boys Ranch twenty-seven years ago.

"Well, hello, Runt," he says.

"Wow! Hey, man, how are you? How's Jenny and your mom and dad?"

"That's why I'm calling. I got bad news."

"What is it?"

"Dad died."

Hardly able to talk, I manage to tell him I'll be on my way to Amarillo for the funeral. I dismiss the class early and go to my hotel room, where I sit by the window and cry.

Five years ago, I went with Tony Kennedy—he of the Blue Max Club incident—to the Boys Ranch rodeo and alumni gathering. Mrs. Price sang the national anthem. Mr. Price worked one of the rodeo chutes. Some of the guys there I'd last seen in the ninth grade, and it was shocking how age does a number on people, like last seeing Opie Taylor and now looking at a bald Ron Howard.

Tony and I, along with a number of ex–Anderson Dormers, met at the Prices' house after rodeo for supper. It's Jeff and Jenny, Kenny Davis and Kent Gardner, Britt Hammond, and several more, including Ty Lightfoot, who we basically adopted even though he lived in Jeffries Dorm. After supper, a bunch of us went with Kent and Kenny across the ranch to Cheyenne and the bluffs where they used to catch rattlesnakes. When it was time to go, time to fly back to Florida, I got teary eyed giving Mr. Price a big hug and saying goodbye. I told him in front of the whole group that he was the greatest man I'd ever known.

Looking out the window of the Holiday Inn, I feel grateful to have been able to say that to him that day, glad I didn't just wave goodbye and not seize the moment. You never know when it might be the last time you'll see your loved ones.

At the funeral, the church is packed and people have to sit in chairs along the back and the sides. Razzberry is here. We couldn't even talk when I saw him earlier; all we could do was cry. Britt Hammond, Kent Gardner, and I sit in the front row. Jeff invited us three to deliver eulogies for Mr. Price. When it's my turn and I go up to the pulpit and face the people, I see so many familiar faces. Mr. Price's mother is here. Razzberry and I used to call her Grandmother Price. She was my pen pal when I was at Boys Ranch. When I look at Mrs. Price and Jeff and Jenny, I lose it and have to take a step back and wipe my eyes before I can start speaking.

I tell them what it was like being eight years old and meeting Mr. Price and how kind he was to me, about the times I would sneak into their kitchen and offer to taste what Mrs. Price had on the stove, about how Mr. Price helped me understand how to better face adversity, and to find my strengths even though I was the runt of the dorm. I tell them when Mr. Price got to heaven and they opened the gates, I bet the whole place cheered for him and celebrated him for what a good man he was and how he spent his entire life leading and mentoring boys at Boys Ranch.

Britt, Kent, and I ride in the lead car with Jeff on the lonely road from Amarillo forty miles north to the Boys Ranch cemetery under Boot Hill. I was the first kid assigned to take care of the cemetery. I mowed it before anybody was buried there; now it's full of headstones.

After the graveside service is over, Britt waits to take me to the airport. Razzberry and I stand off to the side as people head to their cars. I'm happy to hear him report that Kim Reeves at the Boys Ranch Town Office got his disability approved and is trying to see if he can get HUD housing and move to a place of his own. He pulls some papers out of his back pocket, sheets of folded-up notebook paper, and hands them to me.

"Here," he says. "I wrote a couple of poems for you."

"Nice. I'll read them on the plane."

"Don't forget about ol' Razzberry, okay?"

"Not possible."

I head toward Britt's car and call back to him, "One of these days we ought to go on the road again."

"The Salt and Pepper Gang?"

I nod. "We've got a lot of life left, a lot of good times ahead, right?"

"We sure do."

And on we go.

Me and my brother were heading to Dunedin the other day

Going to see Rebekah Pulley, best time of my life

My brother was singing and dancing to the Bee Gees

We laughed too hard to care about life

The road took our minds and we were southbound

Time smiled on me and my brother

We don't see color

And we were headed southbound

Nobody knows where we've been, me and him

Nobody knows where we'll go

Dance fireflies, I need to see your light
Take me to the woods of life
I don't care about this cruel world no more
Dance fireflies
I need the campfire life
Dance for me and my brother
Take us back to our childhood days
Let us run through the woods with you
Millions of stars
Campfire lit up
Us dancing in the light of the fireflies

Here I sit in a sea of tents, a sea of love, a sea of songs
With my childhood brother, soaking up life
All the hippies are smiling at me
I sit by the campfire that warms my bones and leaves
smoke in my clothes
Hear the bacon sizzle in the frying pan
Smell the coffee perking
My brother tells me there's no drama here, no hate, no greed
I never want to leave and go back to the world
So I will sit here with my brother and thank the Lord
For letting us have this time and showing me the real life again

Made in the USA
Middletown, DE
09 March 2021